A Silent Melody

'There is a silent melody making itself heard...'
Abhishiktananda, from a letter to his sister,
Marie-Thérèse, 6 July 1963.

By the same author

Dame Cicely Saunders: Founder of the Modern Hospice Movement
The Changing Face of Death
The Gardeners
The World Walks By (with Sue Masham)
Tutu: Archbishop without Frontiers
Teresa of Avila: An Extraordinary Life
The Road to Canterbury: A Modern Pilgrimage
Beyond the Darkness: A Biography of Bede Griffiths
The Cave of the Heart: The Life of Swami Abhishiktananda
Swami Abhishiktananda: Essential Writings

A Silent Melody

An experience of contemporary spiritual life

Shirley du Boulay

DARTON · LONGMAN + TODD

First published in Great Britain in 2014 by
Darton, Longman and Todd Ltd
1 Spencer Court
140 – 142 Wandsworth High Street
London SW18 4JJ

ISBN 978-0-232-53074-2

A catalogue record for this book is available from the British Library

Phototypeset by Kerrypress, Luton, Bedfordshire
Printed and bound by ScandBook AB, Sweden

In memory of
Jane

… music heard so deeply
That it is not heard at all, but you are the music
While the music lasts.

'The Dry Salvages', from *Four Quartets* by T. S. Eliot

Contents

Acknowledgements

This book has been through many versions and kind friends have read, commented and encouraged at every stage.

I would particularly like to thank Gina and Laidon Alexander, Mary Cattan, Giles Charrington, Julia Cousins, Kate Davis, Stephen Eeley, Judith Longman, Elizabeth North, Marianne Rankin, Donald Reeves, Cynthia Rickman, James Roose-Evans, Larissa Wakefield, Jane Wilde.

Especial thanks are due to Brendan Walsh, Julia Hamilton and John Wilkins for their insistence that I write in the first person, something I found hard at first but came to enjoy.

And to Helen Porter and all at Darton, Longman and Todd, especially David Moloney for his enthusiasm.

Introduction

I have long wanted to write about the extraordinary changes in western spirituality that have taken place over the last fifty or so years. However, the more I thought about it, the more I realised that so vast a subject would demand a doorstopper of a book that would take me twenty years to write and probably find few readers. Eventually I took the advice of kind friends, who persuaded me to approach the subject from a personal perspective, regarding myself as fairly typical of many of my contemporaries. So it has become, I suppose, a spiritual autobiography.

Over the last fifty years I have changed from being someone dutifully familiar with the Anglican Church of the mid-twentieth century, but knowing little about the nonconformist Churches, less about Roman Catholics and nothing at all about eastern religions, in those days dismissed as 'mysterious', to someone who has been involved with much of the spiritual revolution which has so changed our society. I am deeply grateful to live at this extraordinary and exciting time.

I have been privileged to see much of this spiritual revolution at close quarters, not only as a private individual, but in the 1960s and 1970s as a producer of religious programmes for BBC Television and, later, as author of several books, including biographies of figures such as Desmond Tutu and Bede Griffiths, whose spiritual experience is so in tune with our times. So in these pages I turn the spotlight on those aspects of contemporary spirituality that I have experienced myself, reflecting our developing multiculturalism and a new attitude to religion and belief, light years from the segregated pockets of faith that made up the spiritual scene in which I grew up.

To be caught up in the maelstrom of colourful but often conflicting influences leads, of course, to periods of confusion, guilt and lack of identity, but also to a joyous recognition that the people of the world have much in common despite our differences. That while we might belong to different religions, beneath those differences, underlying the institutions, there is a common spirituality. That we share more than we might have first thought and that the deeper we go into any religion, particularly its mystical side, the more we find that the Christian is not so different from the Muslim, or the Buddhist from the Hindu. Or even, one might in many cases say, from the unbeliever.

I also want to explore my conviction that, even in this age of atheism and non-belief, we are spiritual beings. I believe that the human race has an instinct for God, an urge that drives people to search for him.[1] I think the same assumption is made by those who refer to the 'God-shaped hole', an idea first coined by Blaise Pascal when he said, 'There is a God-shaped vacuum in the heart of every person, and it can never be filled by any created thing. It can only be filled by God.' I believe that this instinct, often blind and unknowing, is as deeply rooted in our nature as is the instinct for self-preservation, the need for food and water, the urge to procreate. Not to feel that there must, or at least might be, a God and not to need, sometime in one's life, to explore this possibility, is as unusual as to have no sexual drive or no appetite for food. We are, whether we like it or not, religious animals, who started to worship gods early in our existence and who were creating religions as we painted the walls of our caves. My sympathies are with people like Karen Armstrong, who writes that religion is not something 'tacked on to the human condition, an optional extra imposed on people by unscrupulous priests. The desire to cultivate a sense

---

[1] I hope I may be forgiven for not using inclusive language – it is as cumbersome as it is just.

of the transcendent may be the defining human characteristic.'[2] We, the human race, are a God-seeking people. We are spiritual as well as physical.

So I trace my path from the early 1960s to the present time, my own spiritual milestones becoming springboards into the wider contemporary scene in which I have lived and worked. I want to clarify and understand – for myself as much as for anyone else – the confused wanderings that characterize the spiritual lives of so many of us, living as we do when the comfort of certainty is rarely part of our religious ambience. While there are those who simply dismiss callings from a mysterious world, call themselves atheists or agnostics and put the experience away in a drawer marked 'not proven', there are also many who go through real suffering as they obey the urge to follow a call they cannot resist. We may flee the hound of heaven, but he tends to catch up with us in the end.

My own background is fairly typical of my time. I was born into the England of the 1930s, unknowingly waiting for the Second World War to begin. Our lives were in the country, our play in muddy fields, our exercise climbing the chalky Berkshire downs. Food for our minds and hearts took the form of fairy tales, the classics, Greek and Roman gods and the correct use of the English language. Food for the spirit came, or so it was thought, from Anglican boarding schools and, in the holidays, regular attendance at the village church, which was also, of course, Anglican. For these occasions we wore tidy clothes and tried, usually unsuccessfully, to be on time. We sat diligently through the hymns and sermons, but they meant little to us.

---

[2] Karen Armstrong, *The Case for God: What Religion Really Means* (Bodley Head, 2009), p.19.

We – but perhaps here I should change to the first person, for I should not speak for my siblings on these matters – so yes, *I* assumed we were there to worship God, and indeed I used to sit near a painting of an old man that for years I assumed *was* God, but I saw nothing there of the mysterious being that tantalisingly appeared in other parts of my life and which I knew was there, somewhere, in some form.

So if church and religion did not claim much of my early life, God – whatever I meant by the word – infused every moment. This mysterious being may announce his presence in clear, unambiguous tones, in charismatic experience or even in actual words, but my experience was more a hazy certainty that he (or she, or it – I was not fussy about pronouns) was there, very close to me, surrounding me, filling me. I was not always conscious of this, as I went through the normal crises and sadnesses, joys and sorrows of childhood and adolescence, but looking back I know it was so.

Few people today live their spiritual journey entirely within one religious tradition and while I write from a broadly Christian perspective, other faiths, traditions and practices will be an integral part of the tapestry. So too will the expression that God finds through the arts, particularly, for me, through music.

I will not seek to prove the existence of God – others wiser than I have failed in that attempt and in any case it is not the purpose of this book. I will, however, argue that belief in God can be coloured by what the word means to you. And I may well end up by finding myself unable to use the word God at all.

I hope that this book may contribute to the growing awareness that, even as the sound of church bells becomes fainter, monastic vocations decrease and church rulings are increasingly questioned, we are essentially spiritual beings. And may we never forget that we have rich company and endless sustenance in the books and teachers, the sacred texts and the traditions, the arts and, if we are lucky, the friends, who surround us.

Early Murmurings – Experience

The first murmurings of the yearning for God often come early in life. I remember in that fog of trailing clouds being drawn almost consciously to 'something', though I didn't know what to call it. It was sometimes near, sometimes far, mostly benevolent and always elusive; trying to grasp it was like trying to grasp a handful of smoke. Often after hearing music – I still remember a particularly wonderful concert by the pianist Denis Matthews who came to our school – I went to the woods and sat under a tree, lost in the wonder of it and knowing that such beauty must come from somewhere or someone, it had a source, though I had not the faintest idea what that source was or could be. I must have been an odious little prig, because I remember thinking that anyone who talked after hearing such music simply hadn't appreciated it. The only appropriate response, I prudishly thought, was silence.

It was an Anglican school, so the first formal spiritual milestone of my youth was confirmation, and that stirred up a mental confusion that has not yet been entirely resolved. Three times during my teens I went through the process of being prepared for confirmation and twice, like a nervous horse, I refused at the fence. I felt I didn't know enough, understand enough, believe enough – as if I ever could! The third time I went through with it, but I don't remember it being a particularly profound experience. In fact I remember the white silk dress – I think it was called moiré – that I wore for the occasion better than the revelation of any spiritual truth. There was, however, a strange moment a few days later – one of those moments when you can remember exactly where you were. I was in my mother's sitting room (we used to call it a drawing room, though I never quite knew why), which had two doors; I was standing just inside one of them, turned slightly towards the other. I remember a flash of feeling 'Everything is perfect. There is no such thing as suffering. All is well and will always be well.'

A little later and another experience. I was walking through the woods and I saw a beech tree, its great trunk, its young yellow-green leaves unfurling in the spring sunshine. I knew that the beech tree and I were one and that we were both one with the whole universe. That we always had been and always would be. That experience, brief though it was, has reverberated through my life and has influenced every major decision I have made.

Despite its importance, perhaps because of its importance, I could not, for many years, talk about this and for a long time I didn't even try to do so. But some fifty years later someone I deeply respect urged me to write about it, and – perhaps partly because he was talking to me in the role of spiritual director – I went home and wrote, before my normal inhibitions and reservations caught up with me.

> For over fifty years I have had a companion on my pilgrimage. Seen and unseen, heard and unheard, felt, tasted, smelled – the carrier of my senses, holder of the sacred keys, signpost pointing to my future, knowing of my past, most happy in the now. My beech tree. Or perhaps I should say this special branch of this so special tree.
>
> We met one spring morning in 1948. I was at school, a teenager, walking to a house in the woods to practise the piano. Music was my love, my life, the first way that God

spoke to me. I was probably as happy as I ever was in those sad years, as I walked on the soft leaf mould to spend an hour with music.

How can I tell you how we met, this leafy branch and I? In truth we did not exactly meet, for we had always known each other. But suddenly the great over-arching oneness that was US, unrecognised, unknown, was one. I know that this was true, yet the great oneness was also seen as two – the looker and the beholder. One the unhappy child, standing in the wood. The other tall, strong and beautiful, pulsing with the life surging through the trunk and the branch to the soft, delicate, yellow-green leaves. The branch swept almost to the ground with soaring grace, a generous arm extended, the tip a hand turned up in generous giving; the leaves, still uncurling, wrinkled as new born human babes, the small brown coverings that had protected them still clinging to them, watching their progress into life. And round it, through it, coming from it, suffusing it, was light – the pure white-yellow light of gentlest sun.

We met, we merged, we fell in love – we found each other. To see our oneness we had first to see our two-ness. We had never been two, not really. But somehow the oneness we had once known had gone, so this meeting was simply a re-membering. But a remembering of such significance that it was to be a light in the life of the beholder for all her life.

I shall never forget that experience. But what was different, what changed at that moment? How was life after the Beech Tree experience different from life before? Before I was, in an unconscious sense, one, part of the universe, but unaware, unknowing. I was one in the sense that we are all one whether we know it or not. As a child I was lost in unhappiness for much of the time but for those precious moments, as clear now as 60 years ago, I was somehow in that oneness, in a place of endless joy, where unhappiness was only a word. I had heard the first call of a silent melody.

After this blinding, unforgettable experience, after knowing oneness, came a knowing separation, a lamenting loss, a continual search to know this oneness again. For I had seen *being*, been one with *being*. I had known what oneness – conscious, knowing oneness – was like. I was life and life was me and they were one, I had been one with being, in that place, in that moment, *now* – as we always are in truth, but most of the time we forget and do not see it.

The memory has lasted, it is indelible, but after so many years I wonder if the experience has lost some of its immediacy? So the search goes on, the longing to relive the experience, forever not seeing that it is here and it is now. The beech tree still diffuses its luminous beauty and I am in it, with it, part of it, united with it. If only this experience could be with me always. If only I could realise that, in truth, it is.

❦

So – a glimpse into one childhood and the first stirrings of the longing for God. Those three ways to God – through music, through confirmation, which I suppose one can call ritual, and through nature. They were not unusual, but even when I was quite young I wondered why I was so drawn to this hazy, mysterious world that I later knew could be covered by the word mystical. I remember deciding that it was to do with my parents' divorce.

We are all born into duality, into conflict, but when that conflict takes the form of separated, unhappy, angry parents, where does the child look for peace? I remember in those bemused, unhappy early years, feeling that if the two great archetypes of every child's life, father and mother, were not only separated but disagreed over everything, most of all disagreed over me, then I had to find something in the middle of these warring parents, something that transcended them, that was unchanging, entirely reliable and true. So before I knew the word 'religion', before I had any understanding that I had been born into a family that regarded itself as Christian, I was aware of something. I suppose I called it God, but somehow what it was called did not seem very important. It was the 'something' I had heard in music, the happiness that surged after my confirmation and the inexpressible knowledge of oneness that had been waiting for me in the woods for so long, and that I experienced that spring morning. I didn't know then that I was to spend my life searching to relive that experience; that I was to long for it to infuse my life, to *be* my life, always.

Experience has a special place in spirituality, for not only is experience the starting point of all good theology, but as it often takes the form of mystical experience it can reach the heart of things in a way acquired knowledge cannot. It is true. It cannot be denied. After my life was graced by that single, blessed beech tree I felt I could understand why martyrs went to their deaths rather than deny the truth they had seen in all its blazing glory. Experience is the most blessed friend to spiritual understanding and an indicator that God is at work, though it is an indicator that needs to be tried, tested, followed up with patient practice, for it does not stand on its own any more than one night's passion makes a marriage. And experience can change lives.

We are, naturally enough, most influenced by our own experiences; nevertheless we can also be moved, even changed, by the experiences of others. We can find reassurance in them. Three particularly have touched me deeply. The first one happened nearly seven hundred and fifty years ago.

It was December 6th, 1273, when a middle-aged Italian friar, celebrating Mass, had a mystical experience so profound that he stopped working on the great book that was his life's work and never wrote another word. 'I cannot go on,' he said. 'All that I have written seems like so much straw compared to what I have seen and what has been revealed to me.' Three months later he died. The friar was St Thomas Aquinas.

Aquinas, the Dominican widely considered to be the Christian Church's greatest theologian, had let the *Summa Theologica*, a compilation of all of the main theological teachings of the time, probably the most important work of Catholic theology, studied by theologians and philosophers of all denominations, go unfinished in the face of experience. What a tribute to the value of experience! What a man to act on it! That a theologian as great as St Thomas Aquinas should be able to dismiss his life's work as 'so much straw' compared to the true, direct, experience put theology and theologians in a new light for me.

Some seven hundred years later a young man of German origin woke one morning with the feeling of dread that had been his constant companion for his whole life. He could see no point in living, all he wanted was annihilation. 'I cannot live with myself any longer,' he thought.

'Then suddenly I became aware of what a peculiar thought it was. 'Am I one or two? If I cannot live with myself, there must be two of me: the "I" and the "self" that "I cannot live with." "Maybe," I thought, "only one of them is real."'

He was then drawn into what he calls 'a vortex of energy' and felt he was being sucked into a void, but alongside the terrible fear he seemed to hear the words 'resist nothing'. The young man was Eckhart Tolle, who went on to live a life in a state of peace that has never left him and who has written several books that are having a profound influence on countless readers in the twenty-first century.

Two people, centuries apart, whose lives have been changed by profound experiences. One at the end of his life, leading him to forsake his written work but allowing him to die in peace; the other given life when all seemed lost and using that life most productively. Aquinas changed the face of theology for future generations, yet his experience was, for him, supreme. Eckhart Tolle's gives hope to people in the uttermost despair.

My third example, the one who speaks most directly to me, is from Father Bede Griffiths, the English Benedictine monk who died in 1993. I am drawn to him partly because his first great experience could be classed in the same family of experiences as my own, nature mysticism, but also because he was able to write about it most movingly. I have always felt that, whether he intended to or not, he was writing for people like me, for so long unable to articulate a life-changing experience and grateful for the reassurance provided by his words.

The year was 1923 and it happened when he was a seventeen-year-old schoolboy, walking in the school playing fields. He had often walked this way before; he had seen other beautiful evenings; he had often heard the birds singing with that full-throated ease which proceeds the dying of the day. But this was different:

> I remember now the shock of surprise with which the sound broke on my ears. It seemed to me that I had never heard the birds singing before and I wondered whether they sang like this all the year round and I had never noticed it. As I walked I came upon some hawthorn trees in full bloom and again I thought that I had never experienced such sweetness before. If I had been brought suddenly among the trees of the Garden of Paradise and heard a choir of angels singing I could not have been more surprised. I came then to where the sun was setting over the playing fields. A lark rose suddenly from the ground

> beside the tree where I was standing and poured out its
> song above my head, and then sank still singing to rest.
> Everything then grew still as the sunset faded and the
> veil of dusk began to cover the earth. I remember now
> the feeling of awe which came over me. I felt inclined to
> kneel on the ground, as though I had been standing in the
> presence of an angel; and I hardly dared to look on the face
> of the sky, because it seemed as though it was but a veil
> before the face of God.'[1]

The effect of this experience on his life can hardly be overestimated. From this moment his life was firmly placed in pursuit of the God who had touched him through nature and who he was to seek for the rest of his long life. The experience inspired the lifetime's search of this extraordinary man: he came to regard it as one of the most decisive events of his 86 years on earth. For not only were his senses awakened, but he experienced an overwhelming emotion, a glimpse of the unfathomable mystery that lies behind creation. He began to rise before dawn to hear the birds singing, to stay up late to watch the stars, to spend his free time walking in the country. This sense of awe in the presence of nature began to take the place of the religion in which he had been brought up and which came to seem empty and meaningless in comparison; he longed for these sacramental moments, always seeking a reality beyond the mind. Consciously or unconsciously everything in his life was directed to that end.

And there's the rub: one of the dangers of being blessed with these experiences is that one cannot rest content in what one has received – one wants more. But it seldom happens like that. One of the most moving aspects to the life of Bede Griffiths was that he had to wait for 63 years before he had another experience

---

[1] Bede Griffiths, *The Golden String* (Collins, 1976), p.9.

with that sort of power, and always he was longing for it, searching for it. However, his first experience was a beginning, an opening, an encouragement to start the long journey. It was the first tugging of what he later called 'The Golden String' that was to dominate his life.

And so was mine. And as I write this I realise that my moment of oneness with my beech tree was 63 years ago.

There are no rules about mystical experience, who it chooses to grace, what form it takes or where it leads. There is no logic as to when, or even if, it happens. Some of us strive for years, yet true, profound experience eludes us. It is like coaxing a gazelle to feed out of one's hand – the harder we try, the shyer the creature becomes. Yet to others it comes unbidden and unexpected, in the shower, walking past a London post box, on the road to Damascus. Spiritual experience is a blessing, a random, wilful gift with its own mind about when and to whom to appear: an unexpected gift, appearing in its own time. It is a two-way joy - the longing for God to find a home, the joy of the seeker, reaching, if only for a few seconds, the peace, the security, the love, the oneness, for which we yearn.

The fruits of experience do not stop with the one who has received. St Seraphim of Sarov said, 'Acquire the spirit of peace and a thousand souls around you shall be saved,' and so it is that one person's experience can shed light for others. I have never been a great devotee of the saints – a Presbyterian/Anglican upbringing does not encourage such things - but I am beginning to see how wrong I am. It is their direct contact with the source of all being that gives the saints honoured and special places in the history of humankind. The most famous example of this is the Buddha, whose story has inspired millions of lives.

He was born as Prince Siddharta Gautama 2,500 years ago in the Himalayas. For some years he fulfilled expectations as the son of a king, living a life of worldly pleasure, marrying a princess and fathering a son. Always, however, he was haunted by a sense of the impermanence of everything in this world and unable to delight in it. It was as if something were constantly pulling at him, but remaining determinedly elusive.

When he was 29 years old, he made an astonishing resolve – he determined to find a way to end the suffering in the world. He left home and for six years he led the life of a mendicant, studying under various teachers and following ascetic practices until he was so weak he nearly died of starvation. Still he had not found the answer to his question, still he had not learnt the ultimate nature of things, still he did not know the final goal of existence; most of all he had not reached the enlightenment he sought. Eventually he came to a place now known as Bodhgaya and sat down under a Bodhi Tree there, determined not to leave until he had attained his goal.

After a long and intense struggle and many weeks of meditation he reached his goal. His experience was overwhelming and true. He thought: 'This is the authentic Way on which in the past so many great seers, who also knew all higher and all lower things, have travelled on to ultimate and real truth. And now I have obtained it!'

And others could see it in him. A first-century biography records that a mendicant saw him and said:

> The senses of others are restless like horses, but yours have been tamed. Other beings are passionate, but your passions have ceased. Your form shines like the moon in

the night-sky, and you appear to be refreshed by the sweet savour of a wisdom newly tasted.'[2]

So deep was his enlightenment that, as St Seraphim promised, the whole world was affected.

At that moment no one anywhere was angry, ill or sad; no one did evil, none was proud; the world became quite quiet, as though it had reached full perfection. Joy spread through the ranks of those gods who longed for salvation; joy also spread among those who lived in the regions below.[3]

But for him this was only the beginning. 'Having myself crossed the ocean of suffering, I must help others to cross it. Freed myself, I must set others free. This is the vow which I made in the past when I saw all that lives in distress.'[4]

So the experience of Prince Siddharta led to him becoming the founder of teachings that, in the twenty first century, are followed by some 350 million people; his experience was to lead to the enrichment of generations of sentient beings.

The archetypal figures of most of the great religions were inspired by an experience whose truth they could not deny. Moses heard the voice of God calling from the midst of a bush that was burning but was not consumed. The voice told him to take off his shoes, for the place where he was standing was holy ground. When Moses asked for the speaker's name the voice said, 'I AM THAT I AM', one of the most remarkable statements in the history of our relationship to God. 'I AM' then

[2] *The Buddhacarita*, or *The Acts of the Buddha*, tr. E. H. Johnston (Penguin Books, 1959), p.53.
[3] Ibid. p.51.
[4] Ibid. p.54.

commanded Moses to lead the Israelites to the land flowing with milk and honey, to the Promised Land.

I wonder if there would be any atheists left, I wonder if the word atheism would have a meaning, if we used the term the Old Testament God used of himself? Who can deny 'I AM THAT I AM'? Who can deny the voice of BEING itself?

Many of the great figures in religious history were in touch with this blazing force, a power which finds expression in the great I AMs of the Christian Bible, the ancient Sanskrit mantra 'SO HAM', also meaning 'I am that I am', the Jewish 'YAHWEH', believed to mean 'he who causes to be' or 'he creates' and the single word OM or AUM, meaning without a beginning or an end, embracing all that exists and symbolizing the most profound concepts of Hindu belief.

Yet experience comes in all shapes and sizes. We should never cease to be grateful for the small experiences which pattern and illuminate our lives – they may not save a thousand but experience can be shared, passed on. The first biography I wrote was about Cicely Saunders, the founder of the modern hospice movement. Her experience of dying and death has helped countless people cope with their own tragedies. I remember her ringing me after the death of my husband. In a fit of despair I asked her (the futility of the question eluded me), 'How do I cope?' She was kind and wise as always. 'Plod on,' she said, 'plod on.' Such simple words, but the fruit of so much experience. Plod on – the words struck me with such force that over twenty years later I still remember the relief I felt. Plod on – yes that was all I could do, so I might as well do it whole-heartedly. It helped.

I remember a prayer at school. 'Help us to take delight in simple things.' Oh what wisdom in that short phrase. We do not have to live continually at Force 10 – we would soon be burnt out if we did. In his remarkable book *Holiness*[5] Donald Nicholl tells of Rabi'a, a Muslim mystic who lived over a thousand years ago. One of her followers asked her advice in achieving the virtue of patience, a question which received a two-word answer: 'Stop complaining.' Not only the questioner, but all the others present, expecting elevated guidance, felt let down, but soon, as they put her words into practice and remembered the words 'Stop complaining', they saw the wisdom of her advice.

Some experiences, like, for me, the beech tree, are indelible, never-to-be-forgotten. Others are small, apparently insignificant, not necessarily happy and may not appear to have led to anything, but they are jewels that we treasure, the bank on which we draw, whether consciously of unconsciously. I remember as a child spending hours of the summer sitting in the bows of our small sailing boat. The rest of the family were gathered round the helm, laughing and telling each other jokes, while I would watch the water pass, dragging a finger in the sea, my mind miles away. I cannot claim any great experience, but somehow those hours of nothingness, emptiness, in the midst of laughter in which, for no particular reason, I did not join, have been a source of nourishment, though I cannot tell how.

For many people spiritual experience is the liquor of youth, perhaps returning to grace old age. The middle years tend to be devoted to more prosaic matters like learning a trade and earning a living, to human relationships and sexual joys and sorrows, establishing a home, having a family – in short to the whole huge and exciting world of the phenomenal. Certainly this was true for me. For many years the world took over and

[5] Donald Nichol, *Holiness* (Darton, Longman and Todd, 1981).

spiritual experience hid from me, overlaid, in a sense by my own choice, in experiences of a rather different nature. This is not to say that these more worldly experiences did not have a spiritual component – relationships could hardly exist without a spiritual element, it sings in interests such as gardening, walking and sailing, it colours unexpected moments, murmuring a discreet reminder. But for several years the longing for God was fallow, at rest, biding its time. Or if it was trying to tell me anything, I managed not to hear it.

Experiences leave their mark, as surely as the mark left by spilling a bottle of dye on the carpet never quite disappears, but for some time these early experiences were overlaid by life as a music student in the London of the 1950s: spiritual experience took second place to curiosity about every other sort of experience.

I have never kept a journal regularly but for some reason I have kept most of my engagement dairies – as if to hang on to memories of events, if nothing else. And I am glad I did, for looking through my dairies of the time I am amazed at what fun I had. The fifties are now regarded as colourless, boring times for young people. There are those who say that we were thinking only of recovering from the Second World War, and remind us that the news bulletins were concerned with the Korean War, the Cold War and the Suez crisis. It was a time, they say, when we barely understood the significance of hearing at regular intervals of another African country being freed from colonial rule and greeted the discovery of DNA with dutiful respect rather than an understanding of its implications.

Not long ago I was moaning about today's world to a highly intelligent young nephew and was silenced by his polite response: 'Well, it's the only world I know, and I love it.' In the 1950s I would have felt the same. Certainly it was a time of social conservatism, materialism and affluence, but I, like most of my contemporaries, only took a passing interest in such matters and any interest I took would have taken the form of idealistic disapproval. Simply being alive was rich with excitement. Arriving in London to start my three years at the Royal College of Music I still remember going out that first evening to see the lights at Piccadilly Circus; to those of us fresh up from the country, only a few years from war time blackouts, they were indeed exotic.

If your interests lay, as mine did at the time, in the arts and in culture, there was so much to discover. The Festival of Britain opened in 1951 and thousands of us flocked to the Royal Festival Hall, past the statues of Henry Moore and Barbara Hepworth, where we heard conductors like Otto Klemperer, violinists like Yehudi Menuhin and David Oistrakh, singers like Lisa della Casa, Elizabeth Schwarzkopf and the incomparable lieder singer, Dietrich Fischer-Dieskau.

I remember being one of a group of music students invited to play there to test the acoustics – they were so cool and dead that playing in a small orchestra – I played the viola – you could only hear yourself. I seem to remember that our experience led to reflective chair seats being put in place to warm the sound.

Outside London the Aldeburgh Festival had already started and one year I was lucky enough to be a member of a house party of professional musicians playing there when Benjamin Britten dropped in for breakfast. Back in London I sang in the Bach Choir and went to Madrigal weekend parties, singing the music of sixteenth-century musicians like Gibbon and Byrd with joy. Occasionally I acted as a stringer for *The Times*, writing music criticism – something I did not do for long, partly as I was so ashamed that I should dare to write about, and even criticise, my betters.

There was Glyndebourne, the Bolshoi Ballet and the Royal Court Theatre. *Lucky Jim* was published; *Look Back in Anger* introduced us to kitchen-sink drama and changed attitudes throughout the country, particularly among those unwillingly tied to domesticity. Pinter's *The Birthday Party* divided the critics, the Pop Art Movement began, the first Caribbean-style Carnival laid the foundations for the annual Notting Hill Carnival and the slowly emerging youth culture saw the Beatniks began to protest against the social norms, expressing the first stirrings of the counter-cultural and hippie movements. Mary Quant pioneered the 'Chelsea Look', the first boutique opened in Carnaby Street, Elvis Presley rocked his way to a fame that still endures and Harry Belafonte reigned as the 'King of Calypso.'

The fifties - dull? Not to a student or to someone just starting work at the BBC.

Spiritually it was a different matter. I was not part of any particular group, but I remember the Church of England in the 1950s as confident, 'established' in every sense, and with respectable congregations. I have since heard that some people believe that the seeds of today's decline in Churchgoing were sown in those complacent years, when there was no lay involvement and everything centred on the clergy. Certainly my memory is of going to church only occasionally and only out of a sense of duty – and hardly daring to admit, even to myself, how bored I was by the experience.

In the Fifties where there was any spiritual life it tended to be at the evangelical end of the scale, with Billy Graham pulling in the crowds at vast crusades – in 1954 his meetings at the Harringay Arena topped 2 million. I heard him once at the Royal Albert Hall and watched goggle-eyed as people went up to the front of the hall to publicly declare Jesus Christ as their personal saviour. My inhibitions would have kept me firmly seated even had I been tempted to such a declaration, which I was not. I also remember going to something called LIFCU, the

London Interfaculty Christian Union, and finding that so not to my taste that I did not even stay to the end. Again the emphasis was on standing up and making a public declaration and again I realised this was not my scene, however genuine those who made these statements.

Only one aspect of religion tempted me, but with my middle-class Anglican upbringing and Presbyterian mother that was not something I could, at the time, readily admit to. I used to wander sometimes into a church in west London not far from the Royal College of Music. At the time I thought it was a Roman Catholic Church, so I would creep in, wrapped in guilt, when there was no service, smelling the lingering incense in the air and wondering just what was so different, what was so wrong, about being a Roman Catholic. At the time I only knew one Roman Catholic – a cheerful, generous soul – and almost nothing about the faith. But two things drew me – the fact that T.S.Eliot worshipped here, indeed for 25 years he was Churchwarden, and that Catholics were very sure they were right. Already a lover of Eliot and unimpressed by Anglican vague broadmindedness, I found both very attractive. (It was some years before I realised that this church, St Stephen's, was not in fact Roman Catholic, but High Anglican, albeit as High Anglican as you could be without crossing to Rome.)

So my memory of the fifties was of a full and exciting life in a spiritual vacuum, pierced occasionally by a sweet smell of incense and a guilty longing that I did not understand or even bother to study. However, the next stage in my spiritual explorations was not becoming a Roman Catholic, but something even further from my conventional Anglican background.

2

The Still Centre – Meditation and the Maharishi

'My mission in the world is spiritual regeneration.' Those were
the first words of a talk given by an Indian guru in London in
April 1960. My great friend Jane Davies, at the time teaching
the flute at the Guildhall School of Music, had taken me; she
had already started doing his system of meditation and was so
enthusiastic about it that she was convinced I should hear about
it. I went along willingly enough, but with no great expectations.

She was right – I was thrilled by this strange man, sitting
cross-legged surrounded by flowers and disciples and known
as the Maharishi Mahesh Yogi. I was not in the least put off
by his long straggly hair and his high-pitched laugh. In fact as
I felt the happiness and conviction coming from him and as I
heard about his method of meditation, something stirred; I was
reminded, I think, of those experiences of over a decade ago;
that pulsing inner life that had been submerged in discovering
worlds of a different sort.

All those years ago and I still remember the feeling of
surprise and delight in hearing that meditation is *easy* and
that happiness lies within each one of us. We were reminded
that two thousand years ago Christ had said 'Seek ye first the
Kingdom of God and all else will be added unto you', and we
were being offered a way to enter the Kingdom of Heaven, a
place to which, the Maharishi reminded us, we are in any case
drawn naturally, for who is there that does not want greater
happiness? 'the fish need not be trained to drink the water in

the pond. If it is feeling thirsty it is only necessary to begin to drink. It is as simple as that.'[1]

Slightly to my own surprise I soon found myself becoming one of the Maharishi's followers and tentatively tagging on to the emerging 'counter-culture' movement of the 1960s, a lifestyle that tried to stand for peace, love, harmony, mysticism, and religions outside the Judeo-Christian tradition; which embraced meditation, yoga, and psychedelic drugs as routes to 'the expansion of consciousness', a phrase which was just entering my vocabulary.

Meditation, in 1960, was not a word familiar to the general public and it meant little to me. Its associations then were with the monastery and the convent, it was thought of as something only practised by the devout, the slightly mad and those who had given up the world; it was not something for ordinary folk. Now it was being presented as something for everyone to do, in the context of our everyday lives as what we were learning to call 'householders' – ordinary people with jobs and families as opposed to hermits, monastics, swamis and people in enclosed orders.

The extraordinary man who wanted to regenerate the world, the Maharishi Mahesh Yogi, was an Indian teacher, who came from a Hindu family in Raipur. He took a degree in physics at Allahabad University and in 1941 became a personal assistant to Swami Brahmananda Saraswati, who, after decades of meditation, finally accepted requests to become the Shankaracharya, or spiritual head, of a monastery in North India. He was a much respected holy man and Maharishi, as he himself said, was merely a conduit for the grace of his guru, whom he credited with inspiring his teachings and the meditation technique he taught.

[1] *The Treasury and the Market*, a talk on Meditation by Maharishi Mahesh Yogi (SRM, 1961).

I signed on, of course, how could I resist it? If this was a way to happiness I would be mad not to follow it. I didn't really know what lay ahead except that I would receive a mantra, a word completely unfamiliar to me.

The small initiation ceremony, held in a private house near Victoria station, was known by its Indian name, a puja. An altar had been prepared, with candles, incense, camphor, sandalwood paste, rice, and other offerings in the appropriate ritual containers. I entered the room bringing, as we had all been told to do, fruit, flowers, a clean white handkerchief, and an initiation form. A touch which appealed to me was that we were told not to smell the flowers, for that was a gift intended for the teacher and we must not take it for ourselves: I couldn't work out how smelling a flower deprived anyone of anything, but it was a nice idea. After a few words of worship I was given a mantra considered appropriate to me and taught how to use it. (A mantra, I soon discovered, is a Sanskrit word meaning a sacred word or phrase of spiritual significance and power.) I was told to say the word aloud once, to check that I had it correct, but never, never to speak it aloud again. This injunction had great resonance for me and I remember thinking it gave a new understanding as to why early Christians were thrown to the lions – they would do anything rather than deny their faith. I would do anything not to repeat my precious word. And even now, over fifty years later, I never have.

The method we were taught is similar to the method of meditation found in the Bhagavad Gita, the corner stone of the Hindu faith and a masterpiece of Sanskrit poetry, which is also based on the repetition of a mantra. We were not told it at the time, but later an Indian friend told me about this passage in the Gita, written between the fifth and the second century BC. It certainly bears a close resemblance to what we were taught:

Day after day, let the Yogi practise the harmony of his soul: in a secret place, in deep solitude, master of his mind, hoping for nothing, desiring nothing.

Let him find a place that is pure and a seat that is restful, neither too high nor too low, with sacred grass and a skin and a cloth thereon.

On that seat let him rest and practise Yoga for the purification of his soul: with the life of his body and mind in peace; his soul in silence before the One.

With upright body, head, and neck, which rest still and move not; with inner gaze which is not restless, but rests still between the eyebrows;

With soul in peace, and all fear gone, and strong in the vow of holiness, let him rest with mind in harmony, his soul on me, his God supreme.[2]

Later on there is another verse, which corresponds exactly with what we were told to do when our thoughts wandered: 'Whenever the mind, unsteady and restless, strays away from the Spirit, let him ever and for ever lead it again to the Spirit.'[3] The Maharishi, skilled at using images we would immediately understand, used to say, 'Our thoughts are neither our enemies nor our friends. We simply show them the door and return to the mantra.'

It all seemed very mysterious and commendably personal, especially the choosing of an individual word for each one of us. How did they know what I was like on the basis of a five-minute conversation and an initiation form? How did they decide what mantra to give me? The giving of the mantras is regarded as esoteric, the choice reserved to the select few who have special knowledge, so I have never known exactly how they

---

[2] *The Bhagavad Gita*, tr. Juan Mascaro (Penguin Books, 1962), p.32.
[3] Ibid. p.33.

were chosen. However, I did learn later that the teacher looks at the initiation form and chooses the appropriate mantra mainly by the age and sex of the initiate. It was not really personal at all: there was, in effect, a deliberate effort made to preserve the illusion that the mantras were personally selected. Did we feel mildly cheated? Yes, I think perhaps we did. I did anyway, but at the time we did not want to see catches or mildly dishonest behaviour, we were far too innocent, yearning for this new way to peace and to God.

In return we gave the equivalent of a week's wages – I was a Studio Manager at the BBC at the time and I remember I was earning £9 a week – to the movement the Maharishi started, then called the Spiritual Regeneration Movement. We fully accepted that we should give something in exchange for this great gift: it was suggested that we would not appreciate it, were it simply given to anyone who asked, free of ceremony and free of charge, and I think there is truth in that - it was only later, when the charges became so very high, that questions were asked. We were told to meditate for 20–30 minutes twice a day and to return regularly to see someone called a 'checker' who would monitor our progress. There would also be regular courses, at the time usually held high in the mountains of Austria or Italy, when we would do longer periods of meditation and grow deeper in the practice.

It seemed like manna from heaven. It is true that the Maharishi did not speak very good English at the time and, sitting cross-legged on platforms surrounded by flowers and laughing a lot, he did seem a bit quaint; it is true that he was sometimes over the top in his language and his promises; sadly it is also true that his later behaviour and teaching gave rise to questions which have not yet been satisfactorily answered. But for those who, at some level, wanted a richer inner life and who were not finding it in organised religion, this came like a sigh of relief, for here was a simple technique of meditation that was easy to practise, safe and available to everyone. Almost as important, it was universal – it did not demand allegiance to any particular faith, it certainly did not mean becoming a Hindu. In fact the Maharishi used to advise us strongly to stay with the faith to which we had become accustomed. It was not about becoming something else in terms of belief or lifestyle, it was simply a matter of going within, finding the still centre at the heart of one's being.

In the early days of the Maharishi's teaching his message was simple. Life does not have to be about suffering, he claimed, happiness is the natural characteristic of life. We continually miss it because we go from one thing to another, seeking happiness, but never satisfied with what we find. It is like a thirsty man licking drops of water from blades of grass, not realising that right behind him there is a deep lake from which he can slake his thirst. For this deep meditation was not about concepts, it was a way of leading our attention from the phenomenal, outer world to pure consciousness, to the still place within each one of us. This simple technique of meditation took us through what the Maharishi called 'subtler and subtler' layers of thought, to a state beyond thought, to what he called a state of 'pure Being'. He would use the analogy of the Treasury and the Market – we go to the bank and cash a cheque, which we can then spend in the market. Or he would compare it to a well: you drop a bucket deep down and bring up refreshing, sustaining, water. In other words if we regularly seek the treasury of the Kingdom of Heaven within, then we can go about our day with energy and in peace.

Of course the word 'Being' had resonances with my beech tree experience, but I had never before seen it as something accessible on a daily basis. 'Being' was eventually to become for me, and for many people I know, possibly the most important word in the language and the word that would eventually lead me to a different understanding of the more commonly used word, God.

So I began to meditate with a mantra, twice a day, later becoming a 'checker' myself. This was a very elementary level of teaching. Few of us were qualified to do more than be sure that people were sitting in a comfortable position – usually cross-legged if we could manage that – and that we were relaxed physically. Most important of all we needed to reassure each other about the continual, inevitable intrusion of thoughts. The advice given was simply that when we realised we were thinking about some aspect of our lives – like making a shopping list or worrying about work or our personal lives, or even thoughts about meditation – instead of keeping our attention on the mantra, then we should, as the Maharishi continually said, 'show our thoughts the door and return to the mantra.' We should not feel guilty, merely return to the centre. If the Kingdom of Heaven is sought, 'all else will be added'.

So meditation was very relaxed and easy – in fact it was a pleasure – something one looked forward to doing. Pat, a great friend of mine who became very advanced in this meditation, used to meditate in the car, when she was a passenger. She would just close her eyes and say, 'I am going to have a dip'. Prayer was no longer a kneeling penance, boring and dutiful as the routine Anglican prayers of my childhood had seemed to be, but a time of peace, a time for energy to find its centre. I remember how amazed I was that I would come home from work with just an hour to get supper cooked and ready for friends and thinking I had no time for meditation that evening. But I did my half-hour's quiet meditation, then, miraculously, the remaining half-hour was sufficient for everything I needed to prepare. Around the same period I remember a story of a film director asking the Maharishi if, for the next three weeks, he could be excused his two half-hours of meditation, as he was going to be very busy filming. 'You will meditate for *one hour*, morning and evening,' he was told. He did what he had been so firmly told, doubled his meditation time, and found that never had filming gone so smoothly, never had he had more energy for the work.

I felt totally at home with this meditation, quite undeterred by the meditation's Vedic origins or by the strangeness of the puja. No wonder I felt so at ease with it, for behind the flowers and giggles, the strange words used to describe what we were experiencing, it is in fact very like many of the world's great meditative traditions.

I later came across one such in that extraordinary masterpiece of medieval English mysticism, *The Cloud of Unknowing*. It is said to draw on many traditions, and evokes a transcendent God, beyond human understanding, rather than focussing, as so much Christian religious writing does, on Christ's humanity and passion. There was one particular passage which I read with delight; it says that 'a naked intention directed to God is fully sufficient' and continues:

> If you want to have this intention wrapped and enfolded in one word, so that you can hold on to it better, take only a short word of one syllable; that is better than one of two syllables, for the shorter it is, the better it agrees with the work of the spirit. A word of this kind is the word GOD or the word LOVE. Choose whichever you wish, or another as you please, whichever you prefer of one syllable, and fasten this word to your heart, so that it never parts from it, whatever happens.
>
> This word is to be your shield and spear, whether you ride in peace or in war. With this word you are to beat on the cloud and the darkness above you. With this word you

are to hammer down every kind of thought beneath the cloud of forgetting, so if any thought forces itself on you to ask what you would have, answer it with no more than this one word. And if, in its great learning, it offers to expound that word and tell you its attributes, say that you wish to have it whole, and not analysed or explained.[4]

The similarities with the meditation I was practising were so great – one short word, to be repeated; and if thoughts come, ignore them. How could this meditation feel strange? It was deep in my own tradition. I had been lucky enough to come across a meditation that was, in many ways, part of a universal practice; one which was very similar to meditation in many other faiths.

But reading this passage from *The Cloud of Unknowing* also made me angry. At around this time I had begun the tramp of every 'seeker' - as I suppose we have to call ourselves - knocking at the door of anyone I thought might advise me, mostly priests. Why had no one told me of *The Cloud of Unknowing* and its wonderful, simple practice? Why did they talk of petitionary prayer, intercessory prayer, prayers of thanksgiving, prayers of adoration, but not of prayer that sought simply to rest, wordlessly, in the heart of God?

On a similar line, why was I warned against the writings of the eighteenth-century French Jesuit, Jean Pierre de Caussade? When I expressed interest in reading his work I was so strongly advised not to go near it – by a priest if I remember correctly – that, to my shame, I put the thought meekly away. Later I discovered that de Caussade was famous for his belief that the present moment is a sacrament from God and that self-abandonment to it is a holy state. This belief was to become of immense importance to me, especially through the writings

---

[4] *The Cloud of Unknowing*, tr. A. C. Spearing (Penguin Books, 2001), p.29.

of Eckhart Tolle, but apparently at the time de Caussade was thought to be heretical to Catholic dogma – a mystery I have not yet unpicked.

Being warned off de Caussade seemed in some way related to something else I could not understand – why in those days the Christian Church only spoke of prayer, never of meditation. Now, in the second decade of the twenty-first century, there is some change, but it still saddens me that, with the notable exception of the World Community for Christian Meditation, which teaches the meditation rediscovered by John Main, it is not more widely advocated by the Christian Churches. Back in the 1960s I felt cheated by this clerical disinterest, and my faith in organised religion, already shaky, took another knock.

In those years one of the few Christian priests I met who understood the search of the disillusioned churchgoer was the Russian Orthodox bishop, Anthony Bloom. He was the founder, and until his death in 2003, the Bishop, Archbishop and Metropolitan of the Diocese of Sourozh, the Patriarchate of Moscow's diocese for Great Britain and Ireland – a long title for a truly wonderful man.

His father was a member of the Russian Imperial Diplomatic Corps and his mother the sister of the composer Scriabin. When he was in his twenties he secretly professed monastic vows before leaving for the front as a surgeon in the French Army. He was a tall, well-built and very impressive man, but it was his eyes that I shall never forget. They seemed to see everything, to understand everything. In fact so deeply did he understand that I remember when I had a problem with my eastern meditation, he was the one person who could help - calmly advising me what to do, not even mentioning that perhaps I could do something similar within Christianity. In his case, though, I knew it was not an unwillingness to share the richness of the Christian tradition but that he did not want to shake me from my tremulous hold on this new practice of meditation. In fact, as I learnt more about Orthodoxy I think the help he gave me was based on his deep understanding of the famous Jesus Prayer, when the phrase 'Lord Jesus Christ, have mercy on me, a sinner' is repeated rather as I had been taught to repeat my mantra.

Had I needed more reassurance of the legitimacy of the eastern practice with which I had become involved, or in the similarity I was beginning to see between the Maharishi's meditation and the meditations of other religions, I found it when, during those early years of meditation, I took myself off for a short retreat at an Anglican convent in Kent – one of the few centres of Anglicanism that practised meditation at the time. They gave us each small individual cabins and we spent hours quite alone, simply joining the community for the main meal of the day. I had taken notebooks and piles of paper, convinced that I was going to cover them with the wisdom that would be unveiled to me. I took back notebooks and piles of paper, all quite innocent of words save one small piece of paper, on which I had written 'the darkness and the light are both alike to thee.'[5] I had inadvertently struck gold and had received affirmation that God is beyond the opposites. That too was part of the teaching of the eastern meditation I was practising. I did not realise it at the time, but I had taken the first step into the teachings of non-dualism that were to become so important to me.

Whatever criticisms were later made of the Maharishi, he has earned his place in the history of spirituality for introducing meditation to vast numbers of westerners; he, more than any

---

[5] Psalm 139:12, AV.

other single person, is responsible for the fact that meditation is now a familiar concept for so many people.

For most of the sixties, this meditation was my practice, the background to my life. It was simple and it was, on the whole, good. It gave us a regular practice and it opened the door on aspects of spirituality that were to become increasingly important to me. I made many friends among meditators and went on conferences and retreats; I particularly remember one by a lake in Austria, when we would meditate for up to seven hours a day. There was a memorable occasion on the first day when, before we were in silence, I was rowing a few friends round the lake, rather fast. A Polish friend, far more advanced in meditation than I, said, 'Don't go so fast. You have too much rajas.' So I learnt about what the Hindu tradition calls the three gunas, sattwas, tamas and rajas. They are the equivalent of what we might call 'qualities' and are variously interpreted. Usually sattva is purity, light, harmony; tamas is dullness, inertia and ignorance and rajas, of which I apparently had too much at the time, is activity, passion. Or as a fourth-century Sanskrit philosopher more eloquently puts it: 'Sattwa is buoyant and shining. Rajas is stimulating and moving. Tamas is heavy and enveloping.' [6] The ideal state is when all three gunas are brought into balance in both mind and body. I was beginning to learn the language of the East.

Another memory is of how, when we left the quiet of the lakes to return home, we were advised to ease back gradually in the amount of time we spent in meditation before the retreat ended. And how we were warned that, as we returned to the world, noises would seem noisier, unpleasant smells smellier and so on. They were.

---

[6] Ishvarakrishna, *Samkhyakarika* vv.12-13, 3rd-5th century CE, tr. Gerard J. Larson, *Classical Samkhya*, pp.259-60 (Motilal Banarsidass, Delhi, 2nd edn, 1979).

I was happy to have a practice, quietly relieved that my yearning for God had found an outlet, even if at the time it made me a bit of an oddball amongst some of my friends and colleagues. I remember the amazed reactions to my admission, in those early days, that I had started meditating – 'You can't do something like that, you are far too normal to do such a weird thing', I was told. Whereas now to meditate regularly is as normal as eating fish and chips.

I do not want to give the impression that my early days of meditating were all joy and ecstasy - they were not. I was not one of those who progressed fast and easily through the various stages that were available in the particular system in which I had started. I did not have great experiences, as a few people seemed to have. In fact I was often bored, was not always regular in my practice and sometimes wondered why I was doing it at all. But behind all these negatives there was a deep certainty that meditation was the path for me – that it is probably the right path for many people. But this certainty was tested, when the gentle, wise spirituality of the Spiritual Regeneration Movement was invaded and made famous.

It was 1967 and I was working at the BBC as a producer on Radio 4's *Woman's Hour*. One of the people with whom I worked regularly was the controversial journalist Malcolm Muggeridge: witty, outrageous, for many years a devout and determined atheist but at the time on the brink of becoming a Christian. I asked him if he would like to interview the Maharishi and he was attracted by the idea. But unfortunately the BBC was not. They had barely heard of the Maharishi; in any case who, in 1967, wanted an Indian guru on the air? I returned to Malcolm with the news and to my delight he said, 'Well, let's do it anyway.' Clearly the idea of talking to the man who was to become known as the 'Giggling Guru' amused him vastly.

So we arranged a day, I managed to borrow a BBC tape recorder and we met to record the interview in a house near the Albert Hall in London. Muggeridge was indeed amused, but far more than amused. He took the Maharishi very seriously and when, many years later and not long before he died, he was asked who the most memorable person he had ever interviewed he apparently said 'the Maharishi Mahesh Yogi'. We recorded for about an hour, then, as we left, I promised to try again to interest the BBC in the tape and we parted, he not even expecting a fee, which I appreciated because in the circumstances I was not sure how I could have arranged payment for him anyway.

I was planning to go to Bangor for a weekend's seminar with the Maharishi, so I put the tapes in my case and set off for Euston. When I arrived I was amazed at the number of people there – far more than one would expect, even on a Friday afternoon. I eventually reached the train and met up with my friends, to learn that the reason for the crowds was that The Beatles were on the train, along with other pop stars like Mick Jagger and Marianne Faithful. They were coming to Bangor to hear the Maharishi.

We were assigned various jobs to protect them; I remember I was asked to be sure that Marianne Faithfull did not go topless to see the Maharishi. I was also deputed to act as a waitress for our visitors - they would have been mobbed if they had tried to reach the canteen where the rest of us were eating. I liked them, particularly George Harrison. Somehow I sensed the depth of his spirituality coming through his gentle and polite manner.

So the weekend continued in its surprising and unpredictable way – much of our time being spent keeping the press at bay, or ushering them in for short interviews. It was, of course, a gift to the media. The next morning's *Today* programme carried interviews, the weekend papers were filled with pictures of The

Beatles, sitting cross-legged with the Maharishi, garlanded with flowers and surrounded by guitars and sitars. And yes – when I returned to work at the BBC after the weekend, the world was waiting for my tapes (I never knew how they had got to hear of it) and a 30-minute space was cleared on Radio 4, then still known as the Home Service, for my previously unwanted interview between Malcolm Muggeridge and the Maharishi. So I learnt cynicism with regard to programming. The tape had not changed, nor had Malcolm Muggeridge and nor had the Maharishi, but overnight a pop group had made him famous. And incidentally, Muggeridge's initiative was rewarded and he did get paid!

The Spiritual Regeneration Movement had never seen anything like it and, in another and tragic way, it was a momentous weekend for The Beatles too, for not only did they take the Maharishi's advice and publicly renounce drugs, but they also heard of the death of their manager, Brian Epstein: the inquest revealed he died from an overdose of sleeping tablets. The band knew very well how indebted they were to him; he had discovered them, guided them to mega-stardom and made them the most successful musical artists of all time. Without Brian, most people agree, The Beatles simply would not have existed.

Soon The Beatles, along with Mia Farrow, Mike Love and Donovan and associated hangers on, agents, publicists and admirers, went to India to learn more about meditation. The press photographs grew ever more exotic, and though it was not to be a permanent bond, the connection between the pop group and the Maharishi was indelibly forged in the public mind. It created a huge interest in eastern mysticism and meditation. This was a mixed blessing, as the message was diluted, sometimes even polluted, and the wisdom of the east, as encountered in the West, began to lose something of its purity. A small instance has stayed with me. Mantra – a Sanskrit word meaning a sacred word or phrase of spiritual significance and power – is singular. I remember someone, who today would have been called a 'celebrity', assuming it was a Latin word and referring grandly to his 'mantrum'. A trivial and unimportant example, but it showed the ignorance with which we tried to adopt eastern thinking.

The Maharishi's joy at the publicity he received through the Beatles knew no bounds. His movement now was famous, money was flowing in and it had popular support. But for many of us, myself included, this notoriety held more sadness than joy, for it changed the face of the Spiritual Regeneration Movement almost beyond recognition. Perhaps it was a genuine wish to spread the benefits of meditation, but certainly the Maharishi showed great naivety in not seeing what would happen as he, his meditation and his teaching fell more and more into the hands of publicity people, businessmen - and of course pop stars.

Others were saddened by the changes, including the Beatles themselves. Indeed John Lennon was among those who felt that the Maharishi was too interested in public recognition, celebrities and money. Gone was the quiet yet profound spirituality, its practitioners mostly people who were in some way looking for God, its place taken by meditation as a cure for stress and a technique of relaxation; it was publicised as a route to worldly success and became the subject of scientific experiments. If you like statistics then I can tell you that ten years ago it was claimed that 'more than 600 studies have been conducted in over 200 independent universities and research institutions in 30 countries and published in over

100 peer-reviewed scholarly journals.'[7] Many of these were indeed interesting and made good arguments to encourage people to meditate, but somehow it did not seem in tune with the challenging assertion that had stirred so many of us: 'My mission in the world is spiritual regeneration.'

I think my disillusion was final when I came upon the results of an elaborate experiment proving that if you meditated regularly then your gums would recede more slowly. I have terrible teeth and am all for encouraging one's gums not to recede too fast, but this assurance seemed a long way from sitting quietly and reaching the state of pure being, pure consciousness, which was the Maharishi's original promise. Indeed this change was soon reflected in the change of the movement's name from the Spiritual Regeneration Movement to Transcendental Meditation.

There are now believed to be some 5 million practitioners of Transcendental Meditation around the world – a very impressive figure indeed. Clearly it meets the needs of some. But for me – and for many others – it was no longer the ticket to the Kingdom of Heaven that we had been offered.

[7] *The Growth of Maharishi's Movement:Celebrating 40 years of Success Around the World*, Dr Mike Tompkins, http://pages.citebite.com/i6t7e218cyov

3

A Cauldron of Spiritualities

By 1968 I was neither a churchgoing Anglican nor was I any longer one of the Maharishi's followers. I suppose I could have felt a bit lost, but any disappointment I felt was soon forgotten as I left my job as a radio producer and joined BBC Television's Religious Department: I now had a ringside seat from which to share in the turbulent spirituality of the late 1960s and 1970s.

In the history of spirituality, this was a time of the greatest excitement. It may not have been a profound spirituality, in some cases it was self-regarding and superficial, but with my background of Anglican certainties and middle-class correctness it offered a release into a wider world, a confirmation of my growing certainty that spirituality was not confined to any particular box, but could be seen at work in the teachings of swamis, roshis, gurus and sheikhs; in the New Age as well as in the Christian Church; in flower power, at the time a symbol of a non-violent ideology, as well as in ancient and familiar liturgies. More obviously, and with even deeper significance, I began to learn something of the spirituality of the great non-Christian religions of the world, hitherto largely an under-explored area for me, as for the majority of British people at the time.

It is tempting to look back on these years as a time when the world was young and exciting and those of us who put a tentative toe into the spiritual waters swirling around us were discovering new truths; that we were treading new paths to God, most crucially appreciating the wisdom of the East and making stumbling efforts towards bringing East and West together. In fact a cooler look finds the enthusiasm of the time often slipping over into eccentricity, open-mindedness into lack of discrimination, a yearning for experience into a willingness to tread dangerous paths and to risk losing touch with the base that many of us still had in our traditional religion of Christianity. It is true that western spirituality needed energising, but as astronomy, spiritualism, the druids, Krishna consciousness, Subud, psychosynthesis, radionics, herbalism and, of course, meditation, juggled for our attention, we were offered a rich diet, taking us perilously close to spiritual indigestion. Though the West can be credited with asking questions and making connections between traditions, it was also guilty of popularising and spreading spiritualities without real understanding, rather as the Maharishi deprived his own Hindu tradition of some of its dignity in allowing himself to be courted by money and by fame.

In moving to Religious Broadcasting I had fallen on my feet, for in the tumultuous year of 1968, when students were protesting in Paris and in Grosvenor Square, when the tanks rolled into Czechoslovakia, putting an end to the Prague Spring, and long before Margaret Thatcher turned the word 'choice' into something to be regarded with suspicion, Religious Broadcasting had every opportunity to be relevant and exciting. And far from being mainly the home of *Songs of Praise* – as it had been – or a sorting house for independent production companies – as it became – it was, at that time, a department where you could suggest a programme about almost anything and you would soon find yourself working on it. Oliver Hunkin, the enlightened head of the department, believed that religion encompassed most, if not all, of the human condition, so where were the limits?

The Religious Department had a low profile at the time, and was given correspondingly low budgets; nevertheless I knew that this was where I wanted to be and that there I could explore the areas to which I was so drawn. So for over a decade the

BBC enabled me to see at first hand countless ways in which spirituality is expressed. Looking back, I find it hard to draw up any order or preference; everything was grist to my mill, from whether it was better to pray standing, sitting or kneeling, to whether one could take a real, searching interest in Buddhism while remaining a Christian. So I shall dip a hand into the bran tub of memory and see what I find.

The first day in television I arrived to be met by mild and polite bewilderment. At the time I was a radio producer, I had no knowledge of television or film, and I was a woman, turning up in a department entirely of men, most of whom were priests. I was also, from their point of view, theologically illiterate and approached the work as a broadcaster and a communicator rather than as someone knowledgeable about the world of religion. They simply didn't know what to do with me, so I was summoned to Oliver Hunkin's office, where, with his usual self-deprecating charm, he suggested I went to the south coast, to Hove, to attend an International Conference called 'The Spiritual Unity of Nations'. He was not a typical Anglican clergyman and would, I suspected, rather like to have gone himself, but he knew his duties lay elsewhere and he guessed, I rather think, at the inclinations of this new member of his staff.

So I took off for Hove, with no idea what was in store or what I was supposed to do. I arrived to find the place teeming with people. Forty-one organizations from more than 50 countries were represented, and there were speakers on religion and philosophy, but also on psychology, esoteric studies, theosophy, metaphysics, astronomy and a body called the Co-Masonic Order, which unlike the Freemasons, admits women as well as men. To me it was an eye-opener and light years away from Evensong in the parish church.

My chief memory of the conference was not so much the lectures as of a small room where visitors like me wandered round, surrounded by a circle of small tables, each one attended by someone urging us to embrace their particular brand of spirituality. There was a huge range of spiritual goods on offer, mostly in the form of books and leaflets, sometimes as symbols you could wear or display, always by word of mouth. The stallholders were keen to talk about their wares and I noticed particularly one person, a handsome young man called Nigel, whose looks and the obvious sincerity of his searching was the person everyone, whether the Aetherius Society, the Spiritualist Association or the Order of the Cross, longed to attract. Imagine my surprise when this handsome young man came up to me and said, 'You are a beautiful person.' Of course I was delighted and was just regretting that he was rather too young for me, when his subsequent remarks showed me what the phrase meant – in those days the 'beautiful people' was a term coming from California and referring to the Flower Power generation of the 1960s. I hardly qualified for inclusion, but I was almost as pleased by his assumption that I did, as I had been thinking he was referring to my looks.

The conference was an auspicious start to my new job, introducing me to some of the current manifestations of spirituality and religion that I could – and should, if I were to be the child of my time I aspired to be – be researching and perhaps covering in programmes. It forced me to realise just how limited my idea of spirituality had been and gave me a glimpse into a world of diversity that was as exciting as it was confusing. Were they all true? Were any of them true? How did we know which to take seriously? I'm not quite sure what I learned that day, but certainly my eyes were opened and my vision broadened.

Back in London the most conspicuous of the strange new groups that were beginning to form around us were the young people with shaved heads, saffron robes and japa beads, winding their way through the traffic of central London and singing, singing, singing – it seemed that they never stopped singing. Continuously, hypnotically, they chanted, 'Hare Krishna Hare Krishna, Krishna Krishna Hare Hare.' The words are calling to the Lord for protection and have been compared to the cry of a child for its mother.

Certainly the singers seemed harmless enough, and I never saw any attempt to send them away, even when they blocked the traffic down most of Oxford Street. But I suspect few of us realised – I most certainly did not – that the Hare Krishna mantra is as old as time, that the chanting of the names of the gods in this way is found in the great Sanskrit work, the Upanishads, (which dates back to between 800 and 400 BCE,) and that today the Krishna Consciousness Movement, to which the singers belonged, is accepted by academics as the most genuinely Hindu of all the many Indian movements in the West.

This was the time when hundreds of people, mostly young, travelled east on what became known as the Hippie Trail, driven by the excitement of travel, but even more by ideals fundamental to the hippie movement – seeking God, communicating with other people and, in that ubiquitous phrase of the time, 'finding yourself'. They would start from America or Western Europe, aiming for such places as Istanbul, Teheran, Peshawar, Lahore and Kathmandu. Or they would travel to Turkey, Syria, Jordan, Iraq and Iran and then further east. They returned with long hair, highly coloured clothing and beads; they played psychedelic music and held ideas of free love, simple living and pacifism that shocked some, delighted others. 'Make love, not war' was one of their maxims, 'Turn on, tune in, drop out' another. Sometimes they were hugely influenced by the experience. I remember one young man who was so changed and charming when he returned that I found myself saying to him, 'You have changed. You've lost your ego.' 'Yes, I know. Isn't it wonderful?' he replied.

Were the hippies a religious movement? Or, in socio-religious jargon, a New Religious Movement – a term used to describe a religious faith that is not part of an established denomination? There are some who are convinced that they were; others who say, rather simplistically, that they were not a New Religious Movement because they were not a religion. Some were tempted to make colourful comparisons, suggesting that they are a religion, that LSD is their sacrament and going to hear a pop group like the Grateful Dead is their equivalent of going to church.[1] My own feeling is that they were too vague, too disparate, to be called anything other than hippies, but what is unarguable is that they were exploring areas and facing questions that can be compared to those confronted by people who unquestionably did belong to religious movements.

The experiences of these young people support the belief that there is indeed a longing for God and that, to a greater or lesser extent, we all have it. The hippies had no rulebook or set of beliefs and they regarded churches as hypocritical tools of the Establishment, but they often had strong experiences, sometimes, it has to be said, through taking psychedelic drugs. They needed to understand, to explore, to develop rituals and, just like any group of human beings confronted with a new experience, to find like-minded people with whom to honour and share their experiences.

Some hippies needed to know if there was a God at the heart of their experiences; others had come from families or been to schools where a belief, usually Christianity, was practised and the latent resonances of faith were there to be called on.

---

[1] http://en.wikipedia.org/wiki/Category_talk:Hippie_movement, paraphrase of Viriditas talk 06:58, 9 April 2008 (UTC).

All hippies were considered unconventional, yet many of their values are comparable to those valued by religious groups and many were undoubtedly admirable. They believed in peace and love, they often lived in communes with regular meditation practices and high spiritual ambitions; even the passing of the reefer from hand to hand was done in an atmosphere of harmony and was seen by some to bear a resemblance to passing the communion cup. The hippie life may not have been a religion in the usual sense of the word, but many hippies were genuinely drawn to some sort of spiritual life.

The human race needs belief to be supported by a community and its attendant rituals, but where could these spiritual adventurers go? They found nothing that fed them in the Church nor did the Churches make much effort to accommodate them. We began to realise the sad truth that religion and spirituality are different: that people with well-defined 'religious' beliefs and people who are instinctively drawn to the spiritual are not necessarily looking for the same things. Nor are religious people necessarily spiritual. Professor Robert Fuller, a historian of religion, makes a distinction between the 'outer' aspects of religion, which he says are separable from true spirituality and that 'authentic spirituality, therefore, means dropping out of institutional religion'.[2] Personally I find this a harsh judgement. It may be hard to find, but true spirituality can be found in religious traditions. There are sacred texts, books, liturgies, groups and individuals to prove it.

However Professor Fuller is not alone in this belief that following an authentic spirituality often leads to dropping out of institutional religion, and here lies the beginning of the split, now widely recognised, between spirituality and religion. I was not a hippie, but, as a television producer making religious

---

[2] *Stairways to Heaven: Drugs in American Religious History*, Robert C. Fuller, *Stairways* (Westview Press, 2000).

programmes, I met many by working with them. I am in no doubt that there was in many a real spirituality. The problem was that, finding the Churches could not respond to their needs, the hippies looked elsewhere, often making their own groups, with no tradition on which to lean.

This led into the drift away from the Churches, a split which has endangered institutional religion so much that some think it may soon cease to exist at all. These young people had not necessarily rejected religion, but they were seeking a more personal spiritual awakening: they might try following a new guru, starting a different meditation practice, joining the 10,000 who were initiated into the Divine Light Mission or Beshara, a group which is Sufi in inspiration and involves a great deal of study.

Religion and spirituality are not the same, and I think it is partly this realisation that has made me so grateful for those who carry both in one heart and mind. There are many, known and unknown. Among Christians I would give special thanks to Meister Eckhart, Teresa of Avila, John of the Cross, Thomas Traherne, Jean-Pierre de Caussade, Thomas Merton, Simone Weil, Bede Griffiths, Swami Abhishiktananda ... I could go on. They have the confidence and the courage to stay firm in their faith yet to let their spirits soar. Just as a tree is rooted deep in the soil while its branches reach high into the sky and its leaves are born, grow, colour and fall.

During the 1960s the traffic between East and West became two-way, as gradually the travels of the hippies were mirrored by eastern gurus, sometimes in person, sometimes in stories about them and in their teachings, coming west and adding substance to the colourful gleanings that were becoming part of our lives. The Maharishi Mahesh Yogi was already well established in the

West, and others arrived such as Guru Maharaj Ji, a teenage spiritual leader dubbed by the press as 'the chubby faced boy God', whose organization, the Divine Light Mission, put on a festival in 1973 that attracted huge crowds. There were tales of the controversial, miracle-working Sai Baba, who would produce anything – holy ash, bracelets, even, apparently, an elephant – out of the air, and who was perceived as anything between god-man and con-man. I went to see him later in India and was both mystified and unconvinced.

An even more controversial figure was Bhagwan Shree Rajneesh, a professor of philosophy whose open attitude towards sexuality gave him a popularity he did not deserve. He established a community in the United States but became engaged in bitter conflicts and was criticised for his lavish lifestyle; eventually he was deported. More than any other eastern teacher Rajneesh keys up the extraordinary contrast of someone standing for a teaching that earned him respect, but living a lifestyle that included, in his case, the committing of serious crimes. He was, apparently, denied entry by no less than twenty-one countries.

Whether good or bad, true or false, we cannot disregard the teachings and influences these people had on an entire generation and the way they shifted the religious climate of the West. And some of them had wisdom and must be taken very seriously. For instance Meher Baba, who dictated spiritual messages out of the complete silence he maintained for over forty years: 'Live more and more in the Present, which is ever beautiful and stretches away beyond the limits of the past and the future.' What devout churchgoer would argue with that? Perhaps most deserving of respect was Sri Aurobindo, for the last 24 years of his life also silent. The central idea in Sri Aurobindo's teaching concerns the evolution of life in this world into a divine life. He considered a human person to be a transitional being and thought that the next step in evolution would be from 'man to superman'.

The western educated Sufi, Pir Vilayat Inayat Khan, taught in a tradition that views all religions as rays of light from the same sun. Many times I swam into his orbit, hearing him give lectures and seminars, and always impressed by his gentle wisdom. I never met Mother Meera, widely believed to be an avatar,[3] who had such an effect on so many people when she began giving 'darshan'[4] in Pondicherry. A friend of mine went three times and for over 30 years she remembered being overwhelmed. "She looked straight into my eyes for what seemed like an eternity, then put her hands on my head. That was all. But I felt rejuvenated, calmer, patient and more able to deal with my emotions, for two or three months.'

So too eastern practices came west and meditation groups sprang up. Yoga, already well-established, became even more popular through the work of B. K. S. Iyengar; a Zen group began to hold meetings in London; the martial arts – karate, judo and kung-fu – were becoming popular and their quiet cousin, Tai Chi Ch'uan, was becoming known in the West through the work of Pitt Geddes. I remember using a sequence of Tai Chi in a film I made about the use of the senses in religion – the movements seemed to me so beautiful and expressive. The talented Catholic writer Patrick O'Donovan, viewing the film in order to write the script, insisted on referring to them as 'those dotty ladies' – though when the time came, ever the professional, he found just the right words: in his commentary he called Tai Chi 'the coolest form of prayer'.

Christianity, however, lagged behind. In the early 1970s I was on a committee that needed to find a way to start proceedings at their annual conference. As the subject was religious

---

[3] Divine incarnation.
[4] Darshan: a blessed seeing sought by a devotee visiting a holy man or woman.

publishing, which in those days was, in this country, Christian publishing, I suggested we started on Friday evening by sitting in a circle and meditating together. It did not go down well. One person, a distinguished religious publisher and a devout Roman Catholic, exclaimed in horror: 'But we can't do that. We can't sit in a circle. People might *see* each other.'

The New Age introduced the West to many varieties of spirituality, but for me the most valuable dimension was its emphasis on meditation, which encouraged western Christians to rejoice in their mystical roots; the interiority of the Christian tradition was being rediscovered by the Christian in the pew as well as those in religious orders. The year 1973 saw the start of the Julian Groups, which still meet regularly, all over the country, for silent prayer. Two years later the Benedictine John Main started groups based on the tradition of the Desert Fathers. On his death it was taken over by another Benedictine, Fr Laurence Freeman, and the World Community for Christian Meditation was formed. This is an astonishingly successful and valuable group – there are now several hundred groups in at least fifty different countries. In 1984 the Cistercian monk Thomas Keating started Contemplative Outreach to bring 'Centering Prayer' to contemporary society. Now meditation is practised by most people, whether Christians or not, who are drawn to the spiritual life. No one would today suggest that meditators would be embarrassed to sit in a circle, able to see each other.

Sadly on the subjects of silence and meditation there is not always an accord between priests and people. I have heard many priests say that their congregations are frightened of silence and cannot take too much of it. Even more frequently I have heard lay people admit to their longing for quiet services, with longer periods of silence; they in turn wonder if it is the priests who are afraid of it.

So during the late sixties and seventies a cauldron of spiritualities, from both East and West, was simmering, new ingredients constantly being added as seekers searched and hoped they might find. Today, in the twenty-first century, we take most of this for granted, but at the time there was a constant feeling of the old order changing; a wondering curiosity at what was going to appear next.

There is a delicious irony here. For so long western missionaries had sought to establish their faith in the East, now eastern influences were permeating the West and the clear lines of the Christianity that had ruled in the West for so long was breaking up before our eyes. Choice was becoming endless and confusing, and while the retreat of the Christianity practised by most churchgoing Christians was accelerating, the spiritual scene was alive and colourful and rich with potential. It was arguably one of the most exciting times in the history of spirituality in the West.

4

A Ringside Seat in Television
1968 – 1978

It was this varied and colourful spiritual scene that we needed to reflect if our programme-making was to be authentic and to speak for the sixties and seventies. There were, of course, regular programmes about Christianity – documentary programmes, discussions and the obligatory programmes produced by the Religious Department such as *Songs of Praise*, *Sunday Worship* and the *Epilogue*, a late-night comment on the news of the day. At that time these programmes were firmly under the auspices of those members of the department who were ordained ministers, and though they drew in large audiences, I was happy not to be involved in the making of them. The wild mix of spiritualities that was so enlivening our contemporary life was far more to my taste.

I was amazed and delighted when the first programmes I was asked to produce were a series of three half hour films under the title of *Madness, Mysticism and Drugs*. The idea was Oliver Hunkin's and again, as we sat in his office discussing it, I felt that just as he would have enjoyed the day in Hove, so he would like to have produced this himself. I could hardly believe my luck, having such a subject and such freedom, for here I was, not only being given the chance to work on film for the first time, but being paid to study two states as old as humankind, madness and mystical experience, and also to look at them alongside drugs, an issue which, while not remotely new, was one of the issues that was coming to dominate our lives. So I eagerly started researching this subject, so generously allotted to me by my head of department.

❧

Madness, mysticism and drugs – they all involved the exploration of deep levels of being. And I had the opportunity to immerse myself in them and see if the states they induce have anything in common.

I found myself operating at two levels. First, especially at night, visualising images of these states, colour, whirling circles and patterns, the paintings of Breughel and Chagall alongside disjointed passages of music that sometimes had a curious peace – then, knowing these images must be rooted in something rather more practical, more rooted in actual life experience, I looked at the subject historically. For centuries it has been known that there is something in natural substances like opium and the 'magic mushroom' that induces a state remarkably similar to mystical experience. This was originally found in tribal communities, reaching Europe with de Quincy's adventures with opium in the nineteenth century and Aldous Huxley's experiments with psychedelic drugs, described in *The Doors of Perception*. Later they became the subject of laboratory experiments, spreading to city suburbs and student digs. We in the twenty-first century do not need to be reminded where it led: nor that the drug scene was to become associated with many of the spiritual groups that were springing up around us.

This was, in fact, the most complex issue in making these programmes – there can be a close similarity between mystical experience and the experience induced by drugs. In 1966 a study of the use of psychedelic drugs considered 'average people' (as opposed to severely disturbed individuals) seeking a transforming experience; the writer called this 'the first detailed presentation of a Western-orientated, non-mystical phenomenology' and says that out of 206 subjects, they considered that six had had what he calls an 'introverted mystical' experience. One was a 49-year-old woman who had taken LSD:

> My body became the body of bliss, diaphanous to the rhythms of the universe. All around and passing through me was the Light, a trillion atomized crystals shimmering in blinding incandescence. I was carried by this Light to an Ecstasy beyond ecstasy and suddenly I was no longer I but a part of the Divine Workings. There was no time, no space, no 'I,' no 'You,' only – the Becoming of Being.[1]

Compare that with the famous vision experienced several times by one of my favourite saints, St Teresa of Avila, whose biography I was later to write. She saw a long golden spear in the hands of an angel:

> With this he seemed to pierce my heart several times, so that it penetrated to my entrails. When he drew it out, I thought he was drawing them out with it, and he left me completely afire with a great love for God. The pain was so sharp that it made me utter several moans; and so excessive was the sweetness caused me by the intense pain that one can never wish to lose it, nor will one's soul be content with anything less than God. It is not bodily pain, but spiritual, though the body has a share in it – indeed a great share. So sweet are the colloquies of love which pass between the soul and God that if anyone thinks I am lying I beseech God, in His goodness, to give him the same experience.[2]

[1] *The Varieties of Psychedelic Experience*, R. E. L. Masters and Jean Houston (Holt, Rinehart and Winston, 1966).

[2] *The Complete Works of Saint Teresa of Jesus, Vol. 1*, trs. E. Alison Peers (Sheed and Ward, 1946), p.193.

One experience through taking a substance, the other believed to have been caused by years of prayer and devotion. A world of difference in the means, but was there not some similarity in the experience? The closeness of these experiences, and the sexuality implicit in Teresa's experience, worry many people, especially those who want to make a clear distinction between experiences caused by external and internal means, between spiritual and sexual.

I wish I had tried LSD myself, and it was not good sense or virtue that stopped me – I was quite simply scared. Alarming stories were beginning to circulate about people high on LSD throwing themselves out of windows; there were reports of people who had gone mad as a result. There were countless seemingly innocent stories, which carried sinister overtones of derangement. For instance I heard of a young girl who, in the middle of a drug-induced ecstasy, claimed to have found the secret of life. She was urged to write it down during the experience in case she forgot it. As she returned to normality she found she had written, 'If I stand on tip-toe I can touch the ceiling.'

So an important issue in these films was to consider this question – how the experience reached through drugs compared to a genuine mystical experience. It was a very real question, for even though mystical experiences arrived at through drugs were rare, if it is possible to take a short cut to ecstatic experience with psychedelic drugs, why choose to toil along the long, often painful, route of prayer and meditation? It's very easy for the slightly puritanically inclined (I include myself) to think something is better because it's harder, but Bishop Anthony Bloom, with his usual insight, put it clearly and directly. This was forty years ago but I still remember interviewing him for these films and the certainty with which he said that when you took drugs it was like looking out of a window and seeing something happen. When you found God within you it was something actually happening. He was in no doubt that there *is* a difference, even though a drug experience may be rich and fruitful and may even lead on to what appears to be a true mystical experience.

I was intrigued to find that the same question can arise in moments of ecstasy glimpsed during an episode of madness. I vividly remember one person who talked to me most movingly about this experience. She had had five serious episodes of madness, and during one she had had what she thought might be an experience of unity that had touched her so deeply she could hardly talk about it. I asked her if she thought that experience, when even at the time she knew she was mad, was also a genuine mystical experience. I have never forgotten the pause, at least 20 seconds – and that is a long silence in a television interview – before she said, with total honesty and heart-breaking indecision, 'I don't know.'

This confusion can also be seen in art. There was a Van Gogh exhibition on in London when I was making these films, and I was particularly struck by one of his paintings of cherry trees. I was not thinking of the films at the time, just taking some time off looking at pictures. But this one, which, I did not know (it was not one of the well-known paintings of cherry trees), struck me so vividly that I tried to find out more about it. I discovered that it was the last painting he did before he went finally and completely mad. Was that what I had, at some level, seen? Did that account for the extraordinary power of the picture?

Of course this intrigued me and I wanted to use the painting in the film about madness, so I applied to the Van Gogh estate for permission. It was not given: it was totally and completely refused. There was no way I would be allowed to put on television what, on one level, was just a very beautiful picture of a cherry tree. I still wonder about the story behind that.

The drug scene was part of a phenomenon that in astrological terms was known as the beginning of the Age of Aquarius. I vaguely knew we were Aquarians, whereas the last generation had been Pisceans, but it didn't mean a great deal to me. In fact having been born under Pisces I felt mildly put out at the apparent rejection of my two fishes, swimming confidently in opposite directions. Various dates have been suggested for the time when the Piscean Age gave way to the Age of Aquarius, but one date given by some astrologers is very precise – it is 4 February 1962. On that day, the day the United States announced an embargo against Cuba and nine months before the Cuban Missile Crisis brought the world close to nuclear war, there was a rare constellation of planets when Mercury, Venus, Mars, Jupiter, the sun, the moon and the earth were all found to be in constellation with Aquarius. In addition there were, in certain parts of the world, both solar and lunar eclipses. And, the argument goes, it was then that the Piscean Age ended. Its long reign, over two thousand years, had been characterised by the rise of Christianity, Islam and Buddhism, the age when two fish swimming in opposites directions were seen to symbolise the struggle of the opposites, the struggle of dogmatic Christianity against atheistic materialism, the tension between science and religion.

Whatever the explanation, the culture of the sixties believed that we were entering the Age of Aquarius, the New Age as it came to be called. Awareness of the astrological age in which we were living did not affect the programmes we were making as closely as did the drug scene, but somehow it underlay what we did; it was part of our thinking, even if we were not very knowledgeable about it or even very interested in it. And it was hard to deny, partly because the things forecast in its name were in fact beginning to happen. The Age of Aquarius would, we were told, bring in paradigm shifts in medicine and medicine would become more holistic: this was already true, in fact I was going to a homeopath myself, which in those days was quite unusual. There would be the awakening of a spiritual movement; and there is no doubt that, in its odd confused way, this was already happening as meditation groups were no longer the practice of a few, no longer considered slightly eccentric, but were springing up in living rooms around the country – even in churches. There would, it was believed, be equality between men and women and between races – this too was beginning to happen, if rather slowly.

The fourth and last pronouncement is rather more elusive: it was said that in the Age of Aquarius the collective egoic nature of humankind would no longer be tolerated. This is hard to understand, for while it is easy to accept that the ego needs to be restrained, controlled – surely we will always need to have some sense of our ego, if only in the interests of survival? I find Eckhart Tolle's thoughts on this subject helpful. He argues that ego is identification with form, a collective dysfunction. If we could be free from identification with form, 'Spirit is released from its imprisonment in matter … You realize your true identity as consciousness itself, rather than what consciousness had identified with. That is the peace of God.'[3] And when we see that we all suffer from the same sickness, then Tolle writes, 'compassion arises'.

So perhaps our age is indeed seeing a change in our attitude to the ego, for one of the most conspicuous shifts in contemporary spirituality is the number of people drawn to Buddhism – and the Buddha taught that compassion is essential to enlightenment.

So we were entering the Age of Aquarius, the New Age. A time when eastern spiritual traditions influenced many lives, merging with western spirituality; a time filled with self-help and psychology, holistic health, parapsychology, consciousness

---

[3] Eckhart Tolle, *A New Earth* (Michael Joseph, 2005), p.57.

research and quantum physics; a time when silence, meditation, awareness of the inner self, was sought with a new eagerness. And this New Consciousness, was, whether we were consciously aware of it or not, influencing the programmes we made.

So who were the prophets of the New Age, who did we seek to involve in our programmes? I never met the two great explorers of the psychedelic revolution, Allen Ginsberg and Timothy Leary. Ginsberg was one of the first to experiment with hallucinogenic drugs and it is said that under Leary's influence he took psilocybin mushrooms (also known as 'magic mushrooms') and made a phone call, identifying himself to the telephone operator as God. Leary, a psychology professor at Harvard, was his friend and colleague – it was Leary who coined the phrase so often heard from the lips of swinging Londoners, 'Turn on, tune in, drop out.' The BBC was wary of them and I wonder whether, had any of us had the enterprise to contact them, we would have been allowed to broadcast their views. I rather doubt it, for the story of how the psychedelic partnership of two charismatic and controversial members of America's counterculture sought to promote the spiritual possibilities of psychedelic drugs, which turned on the hippie generation, was hardly likely to go down well in middle class England. It must however be said, that while they sought experience, certainly, drugs were not for them merely an indulgence, they genuinely sought to investigate the human mind.

I did, however, meet many remarkable people – like Alan Watts. He was born in London in 1915, at a very young age becoming interested in the Far East and writing his first booklet on Zen when he was only 17 years old. Six years later he moved to America, becoming an Episcopalian priest for six years before leaving the Church and immersing himself in Vedanta,

Buddhism, and Taoism, though never becoming a member of any organised religion, saying rather charmingly, 'A cat sits until it is done sitting, then gets up, stretches, and walks away.'[4] He became one of the most significant people to interpret eastern thought to the West.

I interviewed Alan Watts in my flat near Notting Hill Gate. I was scared by his reputation and also by the craggy featured face, full of experience beyond my understanding. I don't think I interviewed him very well, all I can now remember was the way he downed an entire bottle of vodka, which he kept by his left foot, but didn't seem any the worse for it. I was more at ease with Satish Kumar, famous for his work for peace and the environment, and Rupert Sheldrake, the gentle, wise scientist who spent a year with Bede Griffiths in Southern India.

Two of the most remarkable women of that time were the poet and expert on Blake, Kathleen Raine and the visionary batik artist Thetis Blacker. Thetis became a personal friend and I would willingly travel some distances to see her colourful exuberance and hear her greeting, echoing across six counties, 'Ah SHIRLEY, how WONDERFUL to see you!' I have seven of her remarkable paintings, and many people comment on how much colour I have in my flat – in fact I think most of it comes from these vivid batik paintings. She herself was twice the size of life and one of the most imaginative people I have ever met. I made a film of her working in her house in Denmark; she was painting a mythical subject, as she so often did – a phoenix rising from the ashes was a favourite. She would stand by the large white sheet to which she would later apply colour, but only when, as she put it, 'the design was still'. So she would stand for hours, watching the imaginary pictures come and go, move and change and eventually settle in her imagination, so lost in it that when someone wearing red jeans brought her a cup of coffee,

---

4 http://alanwatts.com/life-and-works/

she told us later that a red dragon had come into the room, and then left again. And she was not putting it on for our benefit.

I discovered Sufism through Pir Vilayat Inayat Khan, and was baffled by that remarkable Indian – Jamma Krishnamurti, who as a young man had been proclaimed as the Messiah. He had been coming to England for many years, and though only known to a small circle he was becoming increasingly famous through his talks and writings. I recorded an interview with him at Brockwood Park, the school he founded in England in 1969. I had read many of his books and was eager to meet him, but in the event it was a supreme disappointment – not because he lacked wisdom, but that he had so much that I did not know how to converse with him. I sat next to him at lunch – where, incidentally, I learnt the wisdom of serving the salad first, for then one is hungry and does it justice. I was in such awe of him that I did not know what to say, but soon realised there was nothing much one could say, and nothing much that he would answer. It was my first direct encounter with the realisation that the greatest truths are not to be found in words or discussed over lunch. The unfortunate interviewer, Oliver Hunkin, had the same problem, though he dealt with it far better than I, only beginning to learn that wisdom is far deeper than words, and that clumsy efforts to fill silences are usually unnecessary. One could sense the depth of his experience, there was no doubting it. And just occasionally he had been known to find words to express his own profound personal experience. He once wrote:

> I was supremely happy, for I had seen. Nothing could ever be the same. I have drunk at the clear and pure waters and my thirst was appeased ... I have seen the Light. I have touched compassion which heals all sorrow and suffering; it is not for myself, but for the world ... Love in all its glory has intoxicated my heart; my heart can never be closed. I

have drunk at the fountain of Joy and eternal Beauty. I am God-intoxicated.[5]

If we are ever tempted to feel judgemental about those who seek spiritual experience in what may seem strange ways, I find those words humbling and helpful. It's what so many of us want, but we don't know how to find it.

As with all changes, it takes time for new ideas to filter through and become part of our culture, and in this whirl of Carnaby Street, drugs, long hair, walls covered in colourful exuberance, meditation and complementary medicine, Christian voices were not silent, in fact some books of extraordinary power were being written, cutting through the chaos, causing controversy, infuriating some and inspiring others. (Could they too have been influenced by the astrological shift?)

I single out two books, which had a particular influence on me. First the publication in 1963 of *Honest to God*, by the Anglican Bishop of Woolwich, John Robinson. It was almost universally condemned by traditionalists, but hailed as a breath of fresh air by liberals. In this the author, much influenced by German theologians such as Paul Tillich and Dietrich Bonhoeffer, suggested that the ideas of 'God up there' and 'God out there' were over-simplified and outdated. Rather we should join the existentialists in thinking of God as 'the ground of our being'. And what is the ground of our being? Robinson was in no doubt: 'For it is in making himself nothing, in his utter self-

---

[5] Mary Lutyens, *Krishnamurti: The Years of Awakening* (Farrar, Straus and Giroux, 1975), pp. 159-160, quoting Krishnamurti's written account, now in the Krishnamurti Archives, Krishnamurti Foundation America.

surrender to others in love, that [Jesus] discloses and lays bare the Ground of man's being as Love.'[6]

This was a Christianity I could be excited by. I had not come across the phrase 'the ground of being' before but immediately felt at home with it, finding that it resonated with the eastern ideas I was absorbing, though in fact Bishop Robinson makes no mention of eastern thought. He was, however, very aware of the Christian – Humanist debate, another element in the spiritual mix:

> …as I watch or listen to a broadcast discussion between a Christian and a humanist, I catch myself realizing that most of my sympathies are on the humanist's side. This is not in the least because my faith or commitment is in doubt, but because I share instinctively with him his inability to accept the scheme of thought and mould of religion within which alone that Faith is being offered to him. I feel he is right to rebel against it, and I am increasingly uncomfortable that 'orthodoxy' should be identified with it.[7]

For some this was a breakthrough. Rebellion, sanctioned by a Christian bishop. The idea of God as 'the ground of our being', entering our religious vocabulary. Many were touched by these insights, but by the end of the decade the furore had diminished to a quiet rumble and now the book seems to be largely forgotten. A sad fate for a breakthrough in Christian thinking that had been of great significance to many people.

Another book that resonated with me was *Silent Music* by the Jesuit William Johnston, for it marked a change in spirituality that many longed for and that to some extent was already happening – the idea that meditation could and should be part

---

[6] John A.T. Robinson, *Honest to God* (SCM, 1963), p.75.

[7] Ibid. p.8.

of ordinary secular lives as well as for those in monasteries and convents. Johnston had been living in Japan for many years and been involved with interfaith dialogue, especially with Buddhists; he had also become very involved with Zen. I remember recording an interview with him in the basement of the Jesuit headquarters at Farm Street in London. Suddenly, in the middle of the recording, dressed as he was in priestly robes, he jumped out of his chair and landed on the floor in a cross-legged position. Today we would hardly notice such a gesture, but at the time it seemed quite amazing for a Jesuit priest to sit cross-legged at all, and remarkably uninhibited to do it in the middle of a filmed interview.

By 1974, when *Silent Music* was published, Johnston felt able to talk of 'the rise of a great meditation movement which gathers momentum and appeals to men and women in all walks of life'.[8] He accepted that a new age was upon us, that the interfaith dialogue was under way and that 'serious-minded scientists, students of consciousness'[9] who valued meditation and the experiences of the mystics were now part of the scene. He rejoiced, for he felt as so many people do now – and I do passionately – that meditation is the point where the great religions are united. He also accepted the 'paradoxical picture of people meditating night and morning while claiming that they believe in nothing.'[10] And he had a response to the crucial question – was this seemingly agnostic meditation really agnostic?

> Frequently the self-styled agnostic who meditates is searching for something ultimate. And the person who searches believes, or hopes, that an answer exists

---

[8] William Johnston, *Silent Music* (Collins, 1974), p.5.
[9] Ibid. p.9.
[10] Ibid. p.18.

somewhere. In this sense he is not agnostic. Many meditators are in quest of truth, wisdom, ultimate values - things they have failed to find within their own religious tradition. It could be plausibly argued that secular meditation has arisen partly because traditional and established religion has ceased to give people, particularly young people, the religious experience for which they are craving. So they look elsewhere.

Meditation, both spiritual and secular, had come to stay.

Over the next ten years I met a huge variety of people who, in many different ways, were seeking God in a twentieth century which was becoming increasingly non-Christian. There were of course Christian programmes – it was still technically a Christian department – and I reached deeper into the religion into which I had been born by doing films about plainchant in European monasteries, the great service of Easter at the Orthodox Cathedral in central London, and a series of four films about Jesus with Monica Furlong, who was described by the *Guardian* newspaper as the Church of England's 'most influential and creative layperson of the post-war period'.[11] I made a film about Christian Science, where my chief memory is of the stunning hats the congregation wore for the benefit of the cameras. I filmed life in monastic institutions like the Franciscans in Cerne Abbas – where I disgraced myself by asking a group of friars, 'Could you please tell me who is going to pray spontaneously?' (Okay, I needed to know where to point the camera, but that was taking idiocy a stage too far.) I made a film about the use of the senses in religion, another on

---

[11] *Guardian*, obituary, 17 January 2003.

food in the different religions. The Jews, I discovered, had by far the most fun round the dining table, though I was a bit shocked to find that in some households when the (male) head of the house died, his coffin was made of the dining room table – which seemed rather rough on the rest of the family. Where did they eat their sad meals without him? I produced a short studio series on ecology, which was becoming a matter of concern to many people – and a dramatic discussion in which Enoch Powell waved his famous 'rivers of blood' banner and hit the headlines of the next day's press. I was on holiday when it was transmitted and came back to find my programme had made news. I went to work nervously – what had I done?   Only to discover that to make the news is considered an excellent thing in television. How naive I still was! Had I not learnt that from my experience with the Maharishi's interview with Malcolm Muggeridge?

One stream of programmes that touched me particularly was a series I made about dropouts and alcoholics – in fact I became known as 'the department's expert on the seamy side of life'. One, his name was Archie Hill, used to take me round London's down-and-outs, introducing me to them as his wife and giving me the sort of advice I needed – like don't give a down-and-out money, he will spend it on drink – give him a sandwich. This reminded me of the Maharishi's advice – don't give a down-and-out anything – teach him to meditate. Certainly they taught me something, though I still have not figured out quite what it was. Perhaps through them I took a small step forward in the endless battle not to be judgemental, for how could you judge people so unutterably broken by life?

❧

The central point, the one thing I wanted to communicate through making these programmes, was not about different religions. Though I valued the chance to do that, I did not seek so much to widen knowledge of the countless forms that religion can take or to produce visual theology – I was interested in conveying experience, almost any experience. Those moments when something is seen as completely real, completely true. It might be an experience of the deepest mystical truth, as when Carl Jung, asked what he believed, said, 'I don't believe, I know'. It might be the joy of sailing in the open seas, the first signs of spring, tragedy and bereavement, an experience of shame and humiliation.

Perhaps it was in the studio series, *The Light of Experience*, that we most often touched these levels of experience. This programme had its origins in one of those stories of broadcasters and budgets. Peter Armstrong, who had by then taken over from Oliver Hunkin as head of the Religious Department, summoned me, saying that we had been offered a 20-minute slot on BBC 2, but that the budget was only … I can't remember the amount, but in television terms it was pathetic. Could I think up a programme idea for that money?

So began *The Light of Experience*, a series of short, simple programmes, one person talking directly to camera about something that had touched their life. And the courage and the honesty with which they did this was often deeply moving. Out of some fifty programmes that we made while I was the series producer I select three.

Gail Magruder's husband Jeb was sent to prison for his role in the Watergate affair; she and her four young children went to see him each weekend. It is not hard to imagine how nervous they all were the first time they visited, yet:

> We felt as if we would choke because our hearts were so filled with love. Our prayers came so easily. There was no self-consciousness about them, no wondering whether they were acceptable to God. He was right there with us and

we could feel his love. It was the most joyous experience I have ever known.[12]

One of the most remarkable programmes in this series was with Archie Hill. He had travelled a hard road as a drunk, living rough and stagnating in prison cells and alcoholic institutions. He hated God.

> I wanted to meet him face to face, to spit on him, to throttle him slowly with my own two hands. I wanted God to be real so that I could do that to him. My hatred for him was the most intense experience of my life ...

The intensity of this hatred was inflamed by living with his grown up stepson, who was a hundred per cent physically and mentally disabled. 'A number,' as Archie said, 'wiped off God's blackboard.' However, over the years, he came to see Barry's life as one of the purest lives he knew. He had not known malice, greed, spite or self-pity. 'Everything about him exudes gentleness.' So Archie learnt to put his trust in Nature, 'and know that the feeling of heartbreak in the heart of things is but a moment's human hesitation on the threshold of a deep serene, purposeful unknown. And thinking so, I almost touch the peace that surpasses understanding.'[13] I hesitate to speak for him, but I think that through Barry, Archie had learnt to forgive God.

Another one I still remember gratefully was Satish Kumar, who in 1962, aged 26 and inspired by Bertrand Russell's civil disobedience against the atom bomb, undertook a 'peace walk' of 8,000 miles to the four corners of the nuclear world – Washington, London, Paris and Moscow. They were to carry

---

[12] *The Light of Experience* (BBC Publications, 1979), p.56.
[13] Ibid. p.16.

no money and eat no meat. 'Walking taught me that I and the earth are one thing – we are no more separate than my hand is different from me. So this experience of unity was the deep one, the main experience. Now I belonged to everyone, everything, everywhere.'[14]

These three people – and many others, for the series went on for a long time, long after I had resigned from the BBC - had the authority of experience and at this time, the 1970s, with institutions suspect, dogma unpopular and doubt as pervasive as dust, more than ever experience was welcomed and trusted.

At the time it all seemed confusing and diffused, and of course it was. Even now, over thirty years later, I find it hard to see a pattern in the extraordinary diversity; nor am I sure where I belong in the galaxy of choice. But it was just the environment I needed, whether I knew it at the time or not. I was living at the cutting edge of contemporary spirituality, experiencing far more than I understood and unable to refute the charge of 'picking and mixing' that some friends, confident of their spiritual tradition, would politely suggest. It reminds me of Thetis Blacker, watching the patterns change and move until they were still and she could paint. Over these years I met a vibrant spirituality that seemed to be everywhere, and I watched it and tried to reflect it in my programmes. But I was a long way from finding peace or stillness myself.

---

[14] *Light of Experience*, p.27.

5

Immersion in the Roman Catholic Church - John

After ten years of living with my camera lens trained on hippiedom, experiment and choice, life took me in a very different direction – to the heart of the Roman Catholic Church. I married John Harriott, a lifelong, devout Catholic who, until leaving the Society, had been a distinguished Jesuit priest and who remained a deeply valued and significant Catholic layman. Our long friendship and eventual marriage inevitably influenced my attitude to the chaos of contemporary spirituality in which I was living when we met.

His name had been suggested as a contributor to a programme I was making and I went to meet him at the Jesuit Community in Farm Street. A little while later I glimpsed the generosity of the man when a long-standing relationship in my life went seriously wrong. I don't know what induced me to ring him, but I did, and half an hour later he was there, in my flat. He spent several hours with me, refusing to go until a friend happened to ring and invite me round. And he never let me know that he had two talks to prepare for the next day and that he had not written! So one of the first things I experienced about him was that he was an extraordinarily kind man.

In fact he was an amazing man – well you might expect to hear a wife say that, though of course amazing men are not necessarily the easiest to live with – but he was one of the two most widely admired and loved men I have ever known: the other was my brother. I find it so hard to write about him that I take refuge in quoting what others said of him, in the obituaries written after his tragically early death in 1990.[1]

Sir Brian Young, the Director-General of the Independent Broadcasting Authority, where John worked after he had left the Jesuits, called him 'a man of rare grace'. Another colleague wrote that 'truth and integrity were values which he always tried to display and which he expected of others in return'. Father Michael Campbell-Johnson, who was the English Jesuit Provincial at the time, preached the homily at his funeral: 'John was always true to himself, to his beliefs and his ideals,' he said. 'Though he spent 29 years as a Jesuit and 12 as a married man, it was one life, one coherent whole, and John moved closer to God throughout it.' John would have treasured this tribute for he was not a man who could fall in love and leave the priesthood easily. In fact there were many difficult years before we could be openly together.

John was consistently good-natured and cheerful, even when he was seriously ill. The great journalist Hugo Young went to see him in hospital, not long before his death. 'We came to cheer him up. Instead we left enriched by laughter from his soul.' A piece in the *Irish Times* ended with the simple words, so rarely earned – 'he was a good, good man'.

John was the sort of man who gives Roman Catholicism a good name, especially as he had a great ability to convey the truth of the faith he held so deeply. He was once described as 'my preferred mediator between the world I think I understand and the world I know I don't'. His belief that the Church is not a self-preservation society, but a vehicle for God's love and for the cherishing of all humankind drew people to him like iron filings to a magnet. As did his belief that 'The glory of God is a man

---

[1] These tributes are taken from the booklet put together by Bob Towler.

fully alive'[2] – a phrase he loved to quote. Being fully human was, for him, the great goal of life. And he himself was fully human.

This may seem a bit over the top - you may think that I am exaggerating. I assure you I am not. And I am equally sure that these flattering personal remarks would have embarrassed him - in fact he would not have believed them, for he was modest. But the tributes to his writing would have delighted him. On rare days of depression he felt that his columns fell into a void, and he longed to know that he had been read and appreciated, he needed the reassurance. So how he would have loved to read the obituary written by Hugo Young, who said he was 'one of the finest yet most underestimated journalists of his time … The inspiration of many, the salvation of not a few, the source of humour, wisdom and intellectual adventure for everyone who read him.' How he would have thrilled to *The Spectator*, in a piece on outstanding columnists, speaking of John's 'truly beguiling' pieces on cricket, his great passion, and referring to him as 'the late, and very much missed John Harriott - unsung generally, but the "columnists' columnist" as weekly superstar of *The Tablet*'. With characteristic modesty John Wilkins said to me, a few weeks before John's death, that *The Tablet* could afford to lose him, its editor, rather than John, its star columnist.

How I wish John had heard those words.

His influence permeates my life, even now, over twenty years after his death, though I still find it hard to speak or to write of him. He was becoming well-known when we met, so I already knew a little about him and was hugely impressed by something that had just happened before I met him, in 1969. This was the year when *Humanae Vitae*, the papal encyclical banning birth

---

[2]   St Irenaeus of Lyons.

control, was published, and John was one of those brave souls who signed a letter to *The Times* stating that they could not in conscience accept that all means of contraception were in all circumstances wrong. He was the only Jesuit to sign the letter and retaliation was swift. He was removed from Loyola Hall, where he was a retreat director, banished, first to a friend's, then to a convent. He was not allowed to speak about his views, or even to meet people.

This exile lasted for six months, after which a Jesuit friend, Peter Hebblethwaite, gave him a job as a reporter on the Society's journal *The Month*. It was soon after that that he began his regular column, 'Periscope', in *The Tablet*, under the illustrious editorship of John Wilkins. The intolerance of his superiors had unwittingly led the way to his becoming the most distinguished religious journalist of his time.

The matter of *Humanae Vitae* was however a searing experience for him, one that played a part in his decision to leave the Society ten years later and was also influential in turning him from a natural conservative to a radical fighter for human rights. His support of Christian values in the face of Thatcherite materialism, the authority of Rome and the oppression of the Third World, was tireless. He became deeply involved in the work of numerous groups such as the Catholic Institute for International Relations, the Justice and Peace Committee, the Social Morality Council, the Council for International Educational Development and the Council for Christians and Jews. He could not abide the triumph of authoritarianism, whether from the Vatican or from any other quarter.

He had a good instinct, an ability to get to the heart of the matter, whether in politics or in spirituality, and to get it right. Two examples. He was asked to contribute to a book about Basil Hume. His chapter was to be on Basil Hume's spirituality. I was a bit concerned that he did not seem to have much material – speeches, sermons and such like – to read and research, but he did not seem to be worried about it. And when the book was published the universal opinion was that the chapter on spirituality was quite outstanding, in fact the best piece in the book. Here is an anecdote he recalls, when he had an opportunity to observe the new Cardinal at close quarters:

> The event was an informal dinner attended mainly by Catholic laymen from a cross-section of the professions, not much given to hero-worship and, though decently respectful, not inclined to be awed by churchmen however exalted in rank. Like myself, few had any previous acquaintance with the former abbot and there was much curiosity about what manner of man he was. Suddenly he was in the room, a rather boyish figure despite his white hair and black Benedictine habit. And with him came the sense of another presence. My neighbour whispered to me, 'He's brought God into the room.' The remark may sound theatrical but it certainly summed up what the people in the room were thinking then and throughout the evening. And I have heard the same sentiment repeated, in various shapes and forms, many times since. Where the Cardinal is, to an unusual degree he inspires a strong awareness of the reality and presence of God in others.[3]

Politically John also seemed to have an unerring eye. For instance he was one of the few journalists who anticipated Margaret Thatcher's fall. On 10 November 1990, he wrote in his Periscope column: 'It will not be long before Mrs Thatcher jumps or is shot from her blazing saddle.' Twelve days later, she resigned.

Once news emerged that John had left the Jesuits and was available for work, he was head-hunted for his combination

---

[3] Tony Castle, *Basil Hume: A Portrait* (Collins Fount, 1986), p.56.

of experience, tact, knowledge of broadcasting (he had been Catholic Adviser to religious programmes) and writing skills. After much thought, he accepted the job offered by the Independent Broadcasting Authority, later becoming secretary to the IBA's General Advisory Council. One would never have thought of John as a bureaucrat, but he accepted his new role gratefully – it was quite an achievement to be offered such a good job at 45, after so many years as a priest. His initial work was to convene the consultative meetings needed to reallocate the regional television franchises. Though Robert Runcie, Archbishop of Canterbury at the time, and a member of the Religious Broadcasting Council, said he could turn 'the scattered thoughts of a confused committee into sparkling prose', John felt constrained by the limitation of official writing. I remember him telling me that a phrase was removed as being 'too colourful' – he had said that someone had 'earned a place in the sun'. I also remember my own feeling of outrage when he brought home a furnishing catalogue. I almost wept as we sat there, choosing carpets and sofa covers for his IBA office. Were his formidable creative talents to be buried in chocolate coloured cushions and fitted carpets? They were not, of course, and the thought showed my own limitations, not his.

❦

Our relationship and marriage was, in some curious way, written in the stars, and from my side is rooted, I often think, far back in my childhood.

For me, then, Catholicism was another country. My family knew just one Roman Catholic and though we were devoted to her, being Irish, a lesbian and an alcoholic, she was not typical of the people we usually met, and to our rather conventional family, with my mother a non-attending member of the Presbyterian Church, she seemed exotic and different.

In fact all Roman Catholics, viewed – as they were for us – from a distance, seemed different. In those days Catholics were not numerous in southern England, and many of them came from Ireland or from noble recusant families such as the Arundels, the Tichbournes or the Stonors. I was of course impressed by the prominent individuals such as Gerard Manley Hopkins, G. K. Chesterton, Evelyn Waugh and Graham Greene, who had converted to Roman Catholicism – a far cry from some of today's famous converts, some of whom tend to embarrass cradle Catholics.

So how did we see those Christians who used to refer to Anglicans as their 'separated brethren'? It seemed that Catholics genuflected and crossed themselves a lot, had large families and ate fish on Friday. (I could never understand why the most exotic fish was permitted whereas a humble spaghetti bolognese was not.) In those days the women wore black mantillas and young Jesuits like John headed their essays and their letters home with the initials 'A.M.D.G.' - *Ad Maiorem Dei Gloriam.* 'For the greater glory of God.' And of course the Mass was in Latin and the priest faced the altar, not the people.

I somehow associated Catholics with the colour red, though I have no idea why. Had I seen a picture of a cardinal's hat, was it because it is the colour of martyrdom or did red represent an awareness of sin that I recognised as more acute among Roman Catholics than among Protestants? I knew they went regularly to confession, at a time when we had barely heard of the word in a liturgical context, and that they went to Mass when we went to what we called 'Early Service' – except that they went every Sunday and we just went sometimes. Roman Catholics were definitely 'other'.

And they were of course holier than us. I always had the feeling that we were their poor relations, their poor reflections. I admired their Church's strictness, its conviction that it was right, its grand universality – but I was rather frightened of it. It was somehow forbidden fruit. It was not until I left home that I could allow the attraction the Roman Catholic Church had for me to creep into the corners of my life and then it was sometimes to be disappointed. I once sat at the back of a Catholic Mass in a church near Notting Hill in London and came out furious – the priest never looked at us once and I couldn't understand a word he said. I seem to remember writing a note of protest and putting it through the letterbox. I hadn't understood the implications of the Latin Mass as it was then. It was years before I actually took the plunge and became a Roman Catholic myself, yet at some curious level, even as a child, I felt that God was more at home in the Catholic Church than in any other of the Christian Churches.

Given the Presbyterian/Anglican nature of my religious upbringing it still surprises me that when I was about 15 my mother gave me a bound copy of the love letters of Abelard and Heloise, one of the most famous love stories of all time, and somehow intensely Catholic, though they lived in the twelfth century, long before Christians had become polarised into Catholics and Protestants.

Peter Abelard was French, a Professor of Logic, a canon of Notre Dame and one of the most celebrated and controversial thinkers of his time. He was 37 when he met Heloise, a beautiful and learned woman of 19, and fell desperately in love with her. In order to become acquainted with her, he persuaded her uncle, Canon Fulbert, to allow him to become her tutor. Fulbert, who adored his niece and had great intellectual ambitions for her, took little persuading and Abelard moved into the house where Heloise lived with her uncle.

Heloise returned Abelard's passion and the two threw reason and religion to the winds. He would have married her, but she knew the damage this would do his career in the Church and with great unselfishness refused. Even when a child was born and, at Abelard's insistence, they had a secret marriage, she denied she was his wife and gloried in the title of mistress.

Fulbert's fury knew no bounds. He hired assistance, broke into Abelard's room and had him castrated. Shame at his degradation made Abelard unable to face his students and he decided to become a monk, demanding that Heloise became a nun so that no other man should enjoy her as he had. Both tried to sink their love in the love of the divine. Neither succeeded. Theirs is one of the greatest and most tragic love stories, and their passionate letters have survived while Abelard's treatises are largely forgotten.

I have never understood why my mother gave this little book to me. I wish I had asked her. But I am sure it coloured my longings. The image of the passionate, brilliant, sensual monk, the beautiful woman ending up in a nunnery, the story of love frustrated and consummated, of guilt and terrible revenge, lodged itself deep in my teenage soul.

So, in 1979, here I was, after long years of wondering and waiting, married to my Abelard and plunged into a Catholic world. Looking back I wonder if I felt like a cuckoo in the nest? At first I thought that was a suitable image, then I remembered that a cuckoo grows quickly and crowds out everything else. Certainly that was not the case with me. I was outnumbered, outgunned and not even confident of my Anglican upbringing. I was overawed that John and I should be publicly together at last, but I was too dazed, too busy meeting countless Catholics, to think very clearly at all. John was one of the most sociable men I have ever met and I remember in those early days laying the table – for 4, 6, 7 or 8 – straight after washing up the last meal – it never seemed worth putting the dishes away.

Despite my fears, I did not feel excluded by John and his Roman Catholic friends, far from it. I seem to remember putting up feeble arguments in an attempt to stand up for something other than the faith of Rome, but I did not even convince myself. I was very aware that some Catholics might resent me and the part I had played in causing one of their number to give up his priesthood, indeed I rather childishly used sometimes to wear scarlet, a joke between me and myself as I half feared I would be seen as 'the scarlet woman'. In fact they were universally kind and welcoming, many positively pleased at the turn that John's life had taken. One man's surprising reaction on hearing John had left the priesthood was 'Oh how wonderful, now I can talk to him about the Roman Catholic Church.'

Not everyone understood the significance of a distinguished priest giving up his priesthood, (Charles Davis was probably the best known), though over recent years there had been many others who have done the same thing. From my own non-Catholic side I remember, with some fear and trembling, telling my mother that John and I were getting married and that he had been a Roman Catholic priest. So far was she from understanding the Roman Catholic mind that she simply couldn't see anything surprising or unusual in it. Eventually, in an attempt to make her understand the significance, I said, 'Well, there might be a piece in the papers about it'. All she said was, 'That's lovely. I can say "That man loves my daughter".'

❧

Quite recently a friend asked me what it was like to have had 'a marriage made in heaven.' I was startled by the question for I had never thought of it like that and wondered how I had given that impression. John and I had a good marriage, a very good marriage, no question, but it was not without problems. Like any couple, we had a lot to learn about living together. We had much in common, always a good basis: we both loved reading, writing, music, seeing friends, travelling. Our different religious backgrounds were never a problem, more a stimulus to discussion. I didn't share John's enthusiasm for cricket and football and I have never forgotten the occasion when I was not paying attention to some televised match in which Manchester United were playing. 'But it's *my* team,' said an outraged John, sounding about seven years old. I didn't understand at the time, though now I am beginning to. He felt much the same about my interest in tennis, which he considered 'typically Protestant' – by which I think he meant that the emphasis is on competition between individuals rather than between teams. Nor did he share my interest in Jungian psychology – I was in analysis for several years in the 1970s – and I don't think he would have been greatly attracted by Zen, which is now so important to me.

We led very social lives, constantly seeing people, entertaining and being entertained, though we differed in our attitude to friendship. For John everyone he met was a friend or a potential friend. I am less generous-hearted, more selective. I remember saying to him, 'Do you know I think you would like to meet a new person every week' – 'Oh no,' he replied, 'every *day*.' I was quite sociable myself in those days, but that remark left me speechless.

We travelled a lot, mostly in the UK or in Europe. Sometimes I went with him on his business trips to Scandinavia, Seville, or on one occasion a particularly pleasant trip down the Thames, which he spent deep in conversation with a high-powered broadcasting colleague. But most often we went to France, which we both loved and where we felt at home. For my taste, we covered too much ground, never staying long enough in any one place. Looking back I wonder if at some level John knew he was not going to live a normal life span and was unconsciously cramming in as much experience as possible. So my memory of those wonderful holidays is largely of driving, pitching our tent – often in the rain - leisurely picnics, drinking local wines, then dismantling the tent and driving on, to another market town, another cathedral, another simple but delicious French meal in glorious countryside.

Then there was illness. He had always had back trouble, but far worse was ahead. In 1982 he had open heart surgery, which was serious but successful, and he was only just recovering from that when he was diagnosed with a lung condition, fibrosing alveolitis.

This is a progressive disease, so at first it did not affect our lives too seriously, but there were times, too painful to be lightly remembered, when he was ill, sometimes on holiday. One year, when I was writing about St Teresa, we went to Avila, the highest provincial capital in Spain, where the air was too thin for him and he had great difficulty breathing. So there was a visit to a Spanish hospital and a dash home, Madrid Airport being the first time he had to use a wheelchair. The next year we hopefully, perhaps rashly, boarded the ferry from Fishguard to Cork to stay with friends in Ireland, but we were no sooner on board than John again found he was seriously short of breath. I tried to get him some oxygen, but was told we could not travel like that, so we had to get off the boat and take an ambulance to the nearest hospital while, ridiculously, the car, already loaded onto the ship, went to Ireland. Slowly the disease progressed, the dashes to hospital became more frequent and the taking of many pills and the renewing of oxygen cylinders a regular necessity.

They were wonderful times, rich in pain as in joy, but was it a marriage made in heaven?   I think it was, but even if marriages are made in heaven, they are lived on earth, where the rough edges are burnished and differences resolved. That takes many years. Sometimes I see an elderly couple, walking hand in hand,

and I somehow know they have reached that place of unity. We touched that beautiful one-ness, but we were not given enough time together to live it to the full.

🌿

The Catholic Church which I encountered through John was very different from the one I saw from afar as a child, for it had been deeply changed by the reforms of the Second Vatican Council in the late 1960s. Over four years the documents had poured out. As a result of the first, on liturgy, the Mass was to be said in English as well as in Latin. That on the constitution of the Church turned the great pyramid with the Pope at its head into something which could be called a people's Church, a people on pilgrimage, even a modern Church. Documents on ecumenism and religious liberty recognised baptism and religious liberty for all Christians and, in *Nostra Aetate*, the Church's declaration on non-Christian religions, the Council addressed the question of the Church's attitude to religions other than Christianity. Catholics interested in interfaith and the growing number who were practising eastern meditations and drawn to eastern thought seized on this document, delightedly quoting from it:

> The Catholic Church rejects nothing that is true and holy in these religions. She regards with sincere reverence those ways of conduct and of life, those precepts and teachings which, though differing in many aspects from the ones she holds and sets forth, nonetheless often reflect a ray of that Truth which enlightens all men."[4]

This may have been a partial statement, it may not have gone far enough for many people, but it was enough to take the edge of

---

[4] *Nostra Aetate*, Declaration on the Relation of the Church to Non-Christian Religions (28 October 1965).

guilt away from devout Catholics who, in pursuing an interest in other religions, had previously wondered if perhaps they were straying too far from home. The Benedictine Fr Bede Griffiths, who had been seeking what he called 'a marriage of East and West' for some years before this statement was announced, never missed an opportunity to quote it in support of his work.

Many of the people whose lives and thought I came across through John were 'liberal Catholics', an unstructured group of Catholics that boasted such forward-looking figures as Professor Hans Küng, who famously questioned the infallibility of the Pope. The Catholic magazine, *The Tablet*, for which John wrote his much loved fortnightly column, Periscope, is considered liberal and the word has been applied to theologians such as Edward Schillebeeckx, the Franciscan theologian Leonardo Boff, the Indian Jesuit, Anthony de Mello and the Salvadorean Bishop, Oscar Romero, who spoke out on behalf of the poor and in 1980 was assassinated by a right-wing group as he raised the host at Mass. Many of these brave souls were affiliated to liberation theology, which emphasises the Christian mission to bring justice to the poor and oppressed, particularly through political activism. Some liberal Catholics question the need for a celibate priesthood; some support the ordination of women. They are the progressives, sometimes pilloried by traditional Catholics, but figures of immense importance in the Church of the late-twentieth century.

Many of them were disciplined by Rome, particularly those who were teachers and writers. In 1979 the Vatican and the German bishops rescinded Küng's authority to teach Catholic theology, Schillebeeckx's orthodoxy was called into question and he had to go to Rome to explain his views. Leonard Boff was silenced for a year by the Congregation for the Doctrine of the Faith, directed at that time by Cardinal Joseph Ratzinger (who became Pope Benedict XVI); he had accused Cardinal Ratzinger of 'religious terrorism'. Ratzinger was also responsible for temporarily banning Anthony de Mello's teachings within the Church. The Roman Catholic Church was not characterised by free speech.

It was a confusing world and one that deeply concerned John and was frequently reflected in his Periscope columns. On the one hand there were fresh winds blowing through Catholicism, delighting many, disturbing others. Yet within a few years those who seemed to be the bravest, who seemed most surely to be serving their Church and their people and their God, were prevented from doing so by the Church's desire to safeguard Catholic doctrine. It was a side of contemporary Catholicism I knew little about and had not seen before.

As an Anglican, my own position in relation to the Church was obviously awkward. When I went to Mass I was not, officially, allowed by the Church to take communion, but in practice it was more complicated. If I knew the priest and he, realising I was not a Catholic, said beforehand that I could receive communion, then I did. If we were, for instance, abroad, I also did, for no one knew anything about me. But the one thing I knew I must never do was to tell a priest I was not a Catholic and then ask if I could receive communion. Or to turn up at the altar rails when the priest was someone who knew I was not a Catholic. That would put him in a very awkward position as, whatever his personal views on the matter, he simply was not allowed to agree to such a thing.

Many years later, when I was receiving instruction to become a Catholic, I asked one of the priests at the broad-minded Catholic church I was going to whether I could receive communion. He said yes, that was fine. I then said that I was in fact taking instruction and hoped to be become a Catholic quite soon. 'Ah', he said, 'that's different. In that case you should not receive communion now, for if you do you will not appreciate the difference when you become a Catholic.'

I have often wondered about that remark. At the time it seemed very wise and I accepted what he said willingly. But the more I think about it the more I wonder about the implications. I know that Anglicans and Roman Catholics have a different understanding of the true meaning of the Eucharist, but for both Churches it is a sacrament of unity, so may sacramental communion not be shared, as we seek to emphasise our similarities rather than our differences? Does it matter that we are not understanding it in exactly the same way? To eat the body and blood of Christ is so mind-blowing an idea that surely even inside the same faith there are shades of understanding?

In practice, as a person in the pew, I cannot, however hard I try, experience a difference. I never felt any guilt receiving communion from the hands of a Roman Catholic priest when I was an Anglican. And when I eventually became a Roman Catholic I had no problem receiving communion from an Anglican priest.

I could not have had a better guide than John, who never put pressure on me to become a Catholic. So I wonder why, during our marriage, I withdrew from many of the spiritual activities in which I had been involved, why I stopped the sessions with a Jungian analyst which had been part of my life for ten years or so, why my hitherto regular meditation practice had become irregular, why I lost touch with some of my friends from those worlds. Almost unknowingly I had given up these things. John did not expect me to stop exploring paths outside Christianity, but he himself was simply not interested. 'It is as much as I can do to understand Roman Catholicism,' he would say. I think what he was really saying, but did not want to sound arrogant, was, 'I have all I want in Catholicism.' I believed him. But I needed to explore.

Was I drowning in a sea of Catholicism? Sometimes I felt I was, my unformed beliefs and my tendency to wander eastwards did not always sit well with John's fairly orthodox Catholic position. Intellectually I was sometimes out of my depth – I simply did not know enough about the Roman Catholic Church, nor was I well versed in Christian theology. Perhaps most of all I did not have that instinctive relationship with the Catholic Church of those born into the faith, that love/hate relationship that so many cradle Catholics have.

But I know now that my spiritual life was not drowned, it was enriched. I seemed to be living the confusion of so many in the twentieth century, wanting a spiritual life but finding it was, for me, no longer in one place. There was, for many of us, no longer, one faith, one Church, one Lord and Saviour – it had all become more complicated. On the one hand I was living in this solidly secure Catholic home, with a devoutly Catholic husband, on the other were whispers of the East, the esoteric, the strange and curious, the apparently new which was often the very old reappearing, tempting me with other ways of looking at the truth. Above all I wanted the mystical, and though Catholicism is rich in mystics, they did not play a large part in the Catholicism I was experiencing.

❦

It was a long time before I became a Catholic myself, despite my early yearnings towards the Church of mantillas and Latin and incense that I had glimpsed in the 1950s. While John, over the years, had of course been a strong influence, the final impetus came from Meister Eckhart.

I was reading *The Way of Paradox*, a book about Meister Eckhart written by the Benedictine Cyprian Smith. I was so excited about it that I was reading it like a novel, hardly able to put it down to prepare meals. This fourteenth-century German mystic seemed to make sense of many things that were perplexing me.

Cyprian Smith's book starts by reminding us that Eckhart was condemned in his own lifetime but that now, after being largely forgotten for centuries, he was attracting numerous followers from among Christians, both Protestant and Catholic, among Buddhists and Hindus, even the Swiss psychologist C. G. Jung. What was it about Eckhart that was making such an appeal to people of the twentieth century?

The author points out that we are living in an age of transition; that while traditional ways of thinking and living are passing away, new ways have not been found to replace them. There it was, in a nutshell, on the first page. By page four he identified the area in which Eckhart made discoveries so important that he ranks with the greatest spiritual teachers of all time:

> He realized, above all, that the question of God is at the same time a question about Man. I cannot know God unless I know myself. Religion has its origin and meaning in the human heart. Therefore, when the outward forms cease to satisfy, it is only by returning to the human heart that we can resolve the crisis. The sublime and glorious reality which we call 'God', is to be sought first and foremost in the human heart. If we do not find him there, we shall not find him anywhere else. If we do find him there, we can never lose him again; wherever we turn, we shall see his face.[5]

I was hooked. By pure chance (if these things ever are pure chance) I discovered that Cyprian Smith was giving the Easter

---

[5] Cyprian Smith, *The Way of Paradox* (Darton, Longman and Todd, 1987), p. 4.

retreat at Ampleforth Abbey, so while John went with other members of his family to Stonyhurst, the Jesuit College where I too had intended to go, I went to hear Cyprian Smith.

Something resonated, clicked, fell into place and I came home determined to take instruction to become a Roman Catholic. Eckhart had led me to Catholicism.

It was an eventful weekend, but what stays most in my mind is what I came to call 'the Ampleforth Cross'. I saw the Roman Catholics of the world anew, particularly in time and space. Horizontally, I came to appreciate how there are Catholics all over the world, the arms of the Catholic cross stretch from Italy, west through much of Europe and most of Latin America, embraces Asia, particularly the Philippines where over 80% of the population are Catholic, it even has a few friends in India, just 2 per cent of the population.

The vertical arm of the cross was about time. Somehow at the bottom I saw the early Christians, the Fathers of the Church, the great churches of the Middle Ages, the monks working in the fields, Peter Abelard of course, some of the saints like Teresa of Avila … and so on through history to our times, when amid the religious wars and abusive clergy are still seeds of hope.

I didn't feel any more attached to the bureaucracy of the Church, to the Vatican and its Congregation for the Doctrine of the Faith, but something of the world-embracing spirit of the Catholic Church had spoken to me at last. It was not a dramatic conversion. In fact some of my friends wondered what I was doing becoming a Roman Catholic; one friend from school days saying sadly, 'I feel as if you had gone into the next room.' I do not seek to justify what was an instinctive rather than a reasoned action, but I do think the wish to 'belong' had much to do with it. I wanted a spiritual home, a citadel of certainty, a traditional base. I wanted a 'container'. I had wandered for some twenty-five years and I had at last come to realise that even if my wanderings were to continue, I needed a foundation from which to wander. I have often had problems with the Roman Catholic Church but I have not yet regretted joining it.

I didn't tell John immediately that I was receiving instruction – I think it was simply that I had to do this myself and that somehow I knew that it was important for him too that I should do it myself. But in the spring of 1988 – the occasion was a dinner in celebration of my birthday – I told him and a little while later I was received into the Church at the Catholic Chaplaincy in Oxford. My reception was a gentle affair, followed by a quiet dinner with old friends. I had crossed the divide, 'gone over to Rome' as some people say. I remember going to the reception into the Catholic Church of someone I knew slightly: the church was packed and at the end she went round kissing and embracing everyone there. It was not like that for me: I didn't really feel any different. It just seemed the most natural thing to do.

And only that evening did John say, 'Of course the main difference between the Anglican Church and the Roman Catholic Church is that Anglicanism is essentially a religion of this country, Catholicism is worldwide.' Surely his version of my Ampleforth Cross. How typical of him to wait until I had done the deed before he made this remark!

Ultimately the riches I gleaned from those years with John, so close to his Church, did not lie in his knowledge of theology, in his understanding of liturgy, even in his faith in Christ or the boundless good causes in which he was involved. It lay in the man he was, in his very being. And the Roman Catholic Church had much to do with the making of him.

6

The Liminal State –
Pilgrimage

Slowly but inevitably John's lung disease progressed. On 23 December 1990, he died.

What does one do when the world falls apart? There are as many reactions as there are bereaved people. I took the not uncommon route of succumbing to illness and over the next two years had three major operations. Then, as excuses not to get on with my life were running out, hope dawned in the form of an idea for a book.

I had left the BBC in 1978, feeling that if I was to do anything else with the rest of my working life I had better make a move before it was too late. For the last ten years I had been writing, mostly biographies – Cicely Saunders, the Founder of the modern hospice movement, Desmond Tutu, that gallant fighter against apartheid who became Archbishop of Cape Town, and the sixteenth-century Spanish saint, Teresa of Avila. I had been utterly absorbed by all three of these remarkable people and in their different ways they had influenced me profoundly. But even after the two years which bereavement experts say should mark the return to normal living and being, I was still too far gone in grief to immerse myself in someone else's life and my gratitude to Giles Semper, who was then working in the religious department of HarperCollins, is boundless. He had been reading *The Old Road* by Hilaire Belloc and had come up with the idea of commissioning a book on pilgrimage. He invited me to write it.[1]

It was one of those moments of illumination that can appear when life is at its bleakest. After months and months of apathy and indifference I was immediately excited, curious, expectant. It was as if a light had been switched on.

I started reading round the subject and talking to friends and soon realised that much of the power of this subject lay in the parallels between life and pilgrimage. I was drawn to the idea of travelling through beautiful scenery in agreeable company and the deep satisfaction of going slowly, able to feel the earth under my feet, savour my surroundings, but those things could be found in any long-distance walk and there was more to my excitement than that. There was, if I dared admit it, a surging of hope.

My excitement at the thought of making a pilgrimage lay in the symbolism of the journey, the search. Perhaps it was possible, by trudging the long miles from departure to destination, to learn more about the universal pilgrimage, the journey we all make from birth to death. Perhaps this physical re-enactment of the inner search might shed some light on my own doubts and questions, might even heal my wounds and help me to learn to live without John.

So I walked, with three good friends, from Winchester to Canterbury – a road hallowed by time and by the footsteps of men and of animals. A road does not just appear, it is the fruit of long years of trial and error. It is the supreme collective endeavour, a long experiment in which the individual can only be subsumed. And the road is wise. It takes the easiest way, saves us from ravines, bogs and marshes and prevents us from arriving at a river that cannot be crossed, a mountain impossible

---

[1] Shirley du Boulay, *The Road to Canterbury: A Modern Pilgrimage* (HarperCollins, 1994).

to scale. While it may divide and offer bewildering choice, to leave it is to risk dead ends, false journeys.

As I began to reflect on the parallels between life and a walking pilgrimage I thought too of those in whose footsteps we would walk this route between Winchester, once a centre of temporal power, and Canterbury, a centre of ecclesiastical power. There are pagan stone circles, heathen shrines, druid stones and megalithic monuments that show it has been used for thousands of years; later it was travelled by drovers, traders and merchants. It was associated with the Christian pilgrimages of the Middle Ages and is still known as the Pilgrims' Way. Most specifically it was the penitential route taken by Henry II, attempting to expiate the famous remark that has gone done in history as 'who will rid me of this turbulent priest?' The priest, of course, was Thomas à Becket, who was murdered in the cathedral in 1170. Over Christmas, 1903, Hilaire Belloc walked the route, carrying 'no pack or burden' and aiming to arrive on the day of the murder, 29 December.

So there was material here for every sort of reflection. To be lost in history might dull my pain by putting it in perspective; to walk through beautiful countryside with good friends could be nothing but good; and to reflect on the nature of pilgrimage – there lay the real excitement – what might that yield?

The first highlight came early. The Winchester Mizmaze is an ancient turf labyrinth on St Catherine's Hill, just outside Winchester. Though it is not strictly speaking on the pilgrimage route, the Christian tradition has long seen the maze as a symbol of pilgrimage; indeed in the Middle Ages to tread a maze was to make a symbolic journey to Jerusalem. We decided we would do it on its own, before embarking on the pilgrimage proper. An aperitif before the main meal.

I set foot on it apprehensively, wondering what I would experience, wondering whether I would experience anything at all. It is a unicursal maze, in other words there are no choices - if you just keep going you must reach the centre. Almost immediately I was filled with a great sense of trust. I knew that this simple track would not mislead me; if I followed it faithfully I would arrive where I wished to be – at the centre. To and fro, criss-crossing the holy hill, I covered quite a distance and was aware that I was becoming intimately acquainted with the terrain, feeling at home in this intricate weaving. Often, as is the way with the labyrinthine pattern, the path took me away from the centre, but this did not diminish the sense of trust as I went on, almost hypnotically....

Then, so suddenly that it was with a sense of shock, I was there, standing at the centre, a rough log my only company. Did I feel any different having accomplished this small feat? I did, but why? I could not lay claim to any great achievement - it was not far, nor was it hard – but the tortuous path had honoured my trust and led me to the centre. I was filled with a sense of security and wholeness, the one-pointedness of a good meditation. I stood there in thrall, wondering at the effect of so simple an action. Time was suspended. I could hardly tell how long I stayed there, but it was probably only a matter of minutes. Then some children arrived at the periphery of the maze; at the edge of consciousness I heard them laughing and talking as I remained separate, sealed off in my safe, womb-like little world. Suddenly one of the children, spurning the long winding path, scampered straight across the maze and jumped into my pool of quiet, shouting 'I've won!' I was jerked back into the competitive world.

That journey round the maze was a mini pilgrimage. The overwhelming memories are the rightness of that sense of trust and the sadness of competition.

◆

Once embarked on the pilgrimage proper, memories jostle for a place. One of the most significant was also one of the earliest, for on the second day I became acutely aware of the state identified by the anthropologist Arnold van Gennep as 'the liminal state'. He saw this in all rites of passage, which he defines as rites that accompany changes of place, state, social position and age. First there is separation, a detachment from all normal social structures; then the transitional or liminal phase (from the Latin *limen*, meaning 'threshold'); finally incorporation or aggregation, when the passage is consummated.

Clearly pilgrimage, essentially a change of place, is like pregnancy, puberty and marriage, a rite of passage. But what was this state we were supposed to be in – this 'liminal state'? I had never heard of it before and found it strangely liberating to give it a name. It seems that it is an elusive stage, neither here nor there, betwixt and between, on the threshold:

> The liminal state has frequently been likened to death; to being in the womb; to invisibility, darkness, bisexuality, and the wilderness. Liminars are stripped of status and authority, removed from a social structure maintained and sanctioned by power and force, and levelled to a homogeneous social state through discipline and ordeal.[2]

At first reading this passage seemed very theoretical. What had this to do with us? Surely walking across part of south-east England could not encompass such high-flown concepts? But now, in my new role as pilgrim, I determined to relate to the archetypal pilgrim as best I could by simply being myself and

---

[2] Victor Turner, *Image and Pilgrimage in Christian Culture* (Blackwell, 1978), p.249.

seeing what happened; by staying always in the present moment and leaving everything to do with my normal life behind.

To my amazement it was easy. I was already finding that the ties of normal life were loosening and I did not want to use the telephone, write postcards, even think about ordinary life. (This was 1993; had it been later I wonder if I would have felt the same about my mobile phone and email?) Tax forms, electricity bills, correspondence, shopping, social engagements, my garden, friends, even close relationships, must not – and to my surprise did not – occupy my mind; the separation had to be as complete as possible if the riches I was convinced lay in the apparent void of the liminal state were to reveal themselves.

Soon status and authority had gone, and with them many of the roles we usually carry. There was no longer any significance attached to whether I was male or female, single, widowed, married or divorced; I was no longer in the role of employer or employed, consumer or producer, respectable citizen or apprehensive lawbreaker; I had few social obligations other than to my companions. I had no secular responsibilities, no image to maintain, little choice of what to wear or where to sleep. There were no driving licences, social security numbers or pension arrangements in my world and, unlike the children at the Winchester Mizmaze, no feelings of competition. My only ambition was to reach my goal, though how, or even if, I was going to do so I did not know. Lost to the world, I was a mere speck of humanity, stripped of worldly ties, trudging along my chosen path.

It was a liberating experience. Just walking, just doing my best to reach my destination. What freedom there was in this simplicity. I wondered if it might become addictive, if I might never want to live any other way.

Later in the pilgrimage, when we had been pilgrims for some ten days, often walking in a semi-hypnotic state, I found I was living in the here and now with an intensity I had never before experienced. Occupying this tiny point in time and space it was, like the mystical point, infinite. Whatever the minor irritations and frustrations, despite upsurges of violent grief and some very bad back pain, I was, at a deep level, content.

I longed to live always in the liminal state but was not sure how I could do that in the everyday world. As I argued the case with myself I realised there was a sense in which much of life could be described as liminal, interspersed with the high points of rites of passage like weddings and funerals, the Bar Mitzvah ceremony, even the first haircut has been listed as a rite of passage. But of course one cannot realistically be continually detached from all normal social structures, that most restful condition of the liminal state. Perhaps this is why people become hermits, recluses or members of religious orders, who are at least partially protected from normal life. Perhaps it would come in old age; perhaps those lucky enough to die gently can spend their last months or years enjoying the liminal state.

❧

I was much clearer – at least I thought I was – about another crucial element of pilgrimage: the sacred place, the goal of pilgrimage.

A desire to stand on holy ground, to be in a place where the veil between heaven and earth has grown thin, seems to be a deep human instinct. It has been said that every pilgrimage shrine is an archetype of the sacred centre. Perhaps in a sacred place we may experience the transcendent, the 'timeless moment', a universal God, above the differences of religion or denomination. It is paradoxical that we should claim that God is everywhere and yet seek him in special places, yet it is a need that we, having created, have to accept. I wondered whether we are drawn to holy places because we long to externalise the sacred centre within us all. The thought that God is within us is too frightening, we need to locate him somewhere else. But perhaps we need to find God in a particular place before we realise that, if he is anywhere, he is everywhere.

The goal of our pilgrimage was of course Canterbury, and the arrival there was a moving experience. But there were other places where the sense of the sacred was almost overwhelming. A cathedral of beech trees on the North Downs, where I was overcome with such a feeling of awe that it was as if we had already reached our goal. Then there was St Mary's Church, Eastwell, just off the Pilgrim's Way. There is the deepest sense of peace among its graceful ruins and I was touched by the notice on the church tower: 'This ancient house of God is being repaired by the Friends of Friendless Churches … It remains a consecrated building and the churchyard is sacred ground. Please respect them accordingly.' We did.

The place that was for me most imbued by a sense of the sacred was, however, the Coldrum Stones.

We were on a particularly beautiful stretch of the North Downs Way, walking physically separately yet in amiable companionship. There were woods on the hills above us, exuberant arable fields to our right, chalk underfoot and, as always, cow parsley embroidering the verges. We passed Platt Hill Wood, Hognore Wood and a house appropriately named Pilgrim House, from where we could see Trottiscliffe Church, which by then we knew was pronounced 'Trosley'. Then we walked along the south side of Great Wood until we reached the turning to the Coldrum Stones, which lie just half a mile off the Pilgrims' Way.

I had been longing for this moment; I had visited the Coldrum Stones before and found the site infinitely moving. It is a Neolithic long barrow, and in 1910 excavators found the bones of 22 people, men, women and children, some of which were taken to Trottiscliffe Church. The bones revealed that these people were short and strong in stature, with long heads and broad feet. The bones of ox, cat, deer, rabbit and fox suggest that they were meat eaters and their teeth were healthy, but the elderly apparently suffered from rheumatism and all the shin bones were flattened by the squatting posture they favoured. They were members of the Neolithic farming community who were the first to settle in this part of Kent and these twenty-two people were among the most prestigious of the community, possibly even members of a royal family.

Careful study of the barrow and the bones during the excavation suggested that the bodies of the dead were laid in a separate wooden structure until the flesh had rotted, then when the bones fell apart, they were gathered up, separated and placed in the tombs with great care. Though the religious beliefs of Neolithic farming communities are not known, experts believe that the planning and thought given to these long barrows speak of well-organised communities with a belief in some sort of life after death. To anyone interested in the universal symbolism underlying different religions, it is interesting that the larger end of long barrows, containing the main sepulchre, frequently point, as do the altars of Christian churches, in an easterly direction. The distinguished archeologist Jacquetta Hawkes goes further, suggesting that these monuments must have served as religious meeting places and that the cult associated with the tombs was concerned with ideas of rebirth.

I do not think it is allowing the imagination too great liberty to say that the faith, for it was very truly a faith, which made the New Stone Age communities labour to drag, raise, pile thousands of tons of stone and earth, was in resurrection, the resurrection of their corn and beasts, of themselves. They laid their dead in the dark chamber with something of the same conviction with which they cast the seed corn into the soil.[3]

---

[3] Jacquetta Hawkes, *A Guide to the Prehistoric and Roman Monuments in England and Wales* (Chatto and Windus, 1951), p.49.

I have never understood why some Christians are threatened by pre-Christian religions, by the fact that there were crucified saviours before Christ, that the idea of the Trinity appeared in Egyptian and Indian religions long before Christianity and that, as Jacquetta Hawkes writes, the idea of resurrection goes back to the Stone Age and probably beyond. That Christianity draws on earlier religions, which themselves draw deep from the human psyche, seems to me to confirm the depth of its wisdom.

As we neared the site I wondered if this ancient place would strike me again with the force of my first visit. There they still were, the massive stones, four standing upright in the centre, many more fallen to the ground in a peristalith, a stone circle. The light was bright, the wind blustering around as it had blustered for four thousand years; the grass mown close and clean, the simple fence surrounding the burial chamber discreet and solid. Knowing almost nothing about this family with my head, to my heart they seemed familiar and loveable. I was tempted to get closer to those far-off ancestors; it was respect that prevented me. I felt the need to cross myself, restrained again by respect for the pagan bones, whose God may not have wanted that particular action. This was a pilgrimage in itself. This was holy ground.

Too moved for discussion, we stayed silently for some time. I was standing at the back of the circle of stones, looking east, when suddenly I saw, in the far distance and exactly above the central stone, the spire of Birling church. It was a wonderful moment of completion. The burial chamber, built by pagans seeking resurrection in their way; the Christian church, proclaiming the resurrection of Christ.

*

And where was John, as I walked? He was never far away, but he took different forms in my mind. Sometimes the pain was too much. There was one lunchtime when one of my companions went to phone her husband and came back saying to another married companion in a 'we-wives-together' sort of way, 'There's a phone over there, by the garage.' I should say that normally I was not put out by my married companions phoning home, but on this occasion, for no particular reason, I could not bear it and the knowledge that I could not ring John struck me with such excruciating pain that I beat a hasty retreat to the Ladies. There I howled – long, without control and, I'm afraid, noisily. Eventually a voice from the next-door cubicle said, 'Are you all right?' as people do. And as people do, I lied, 'Yes, thank you.' The voice said, 'It'll pass, I've been there.' Ordinary words, but I was comforted. I am still grateful to that kind person.

There were other times when I was powerfully assailed by his presence and by the knowledge that he was there somewhere, looking after me. He was not just in my mind, but with me on the path, in benevolent and loving control. It was both infinitely sad and curiously reassuring. But I was not finding it easy to learn how to relate to the most important person in my life when he was no longer with me in physical form.

If you are lucky there are moments on a pilgrimage, indeed on any walk, where there are no stiles to scramble over, no need to consult maps or to wonder if you are on the right path, when the going is easy. Then we could move with the rhythmic continuity for which I longed. Walking becomes a meditation. A gentle attuning to the rhythm of the earth. There was now no doubt that we were indeed pilgrims, not just long-distance walkers out on a day's hike. There was space for reflection, for entering into the minds of other pilgrims.

This happened for us quite often, but one occasion I particularly remember was soon after we reached Kent. I found myself thinking not only of the medieval pilgrims, but of the early Celtic Christians, setting out to journey for God. Their trust was quite astonishing:

> They were emulating Abraham, who left his settled homeland at the command of Yahweh, and like him they made no plans but trusted that God would direct their footsteps. We are told that they even went to sea rudderless, letting the currents, the tides, and the winds take them to a destination known only to God.[4]

A destination known only to God; a journey without a goal. The thought of these Celts, rudderless on the open sea, threw into stark relief another question so often in my mind – which is more important, the journey or the arrival?

My instinct was still, as it had been before we set out, that it was the journey, that Robert Louis Stevenson was right when he said 'To travel hopefully is a better thing than to arrive.' We may long for the still centre, we may agree with St Augustine that 'Our hearts are restless till they rest in Thee', but while we are on this earth our human nature is to move, through time and across distance; we age, change and develop. The physical movement of pilgrimage symbolises purposefulness. It is an attempt to find meaning, an incarnation of the inner journey. I think this is why it was so important to me to walk the whole way and not to take lifts or skip stretches of road that might not seem very inviting. The parallels between the two journeys mean that to cheat in one carries the implication that one would be prepared to cheat in the other.

But if the journey is the more important, what of the arrival, the goal? Would I mind if I did not actually arrive at my destination? I knew that I would, that the sense of anti-climax

---

4 Shirley Toulson, *The Celtic Year* (Element Books, 1993), p.118.

would be terrible, but if this were to be a true pilgrimage I knew that I would rather fail to reach Canterbury than miss even a mile of the physical effort. It seemed immensely important to walk every step. I suppose this conviction bordered on neurosis when, realising we had somehow missed a mile or two, I insisted on going back, finding the right path and retracing my steps on the true route.

The act of pilgrimage and the sacred place are, like all journeys and all arrivals, intertwined. There can be no Way of the Cross if there is no crucifixion; even the rudderless Celts would eventually have arrived somewhere. I began to think that perhaps journeying and arriving reflect different parts of ourselves, especially when I discovered that some people strongly resist the idea that the journey might be more important than the arrival. I liked the reaction of a friend I mentioned this to. 'Journeying', he said, 'has liberal overtones. It is in the exploration mode, agonising, wondering, doubting and lost. As opposed to a conservative attitude, about confidence, certainty and arrival.' I liked, too, a saying of the sixth-century philosopher Boethius, which, at least for Christians, should put an end to discussion, 'Thou art the journey and the journey's end!'[5]

❦

Perhaps we should all have travelled the last two miles to the cathedral together, a band of pilgrims reaching our goal, but my wish to walk alone was strong, also I wanted to leave plenty of time to wander round the cathedral before Evensong at 3.30, so I asked my companions if they would mind if I set off on my own. I discovered later that one of them did, a little, but I'm afraid that selfishness won the day and I set off. Across a

---

[5] Quoted in *Prayers for Pilgrims*, ed. Margaret Pawley (SPCK, 1991), p. 18.

roundabout, onto the London Road, past the Pilgrim Hospice, along Saint Dunstan's Street and into the Westgate. All the way I was in a state of such excitement and apprehension that I hardly took in my surroundings. I suppose it was fear of arrival being an anti-climax that was at the root of my nervousness, but I was filled with extravagant and absurd thoughts. I felt as if I was approaching life itself – or was it death?

My fears took more concrete form as I became convinced that now, at the eleventh hour, something was going to prevent me reaching the shrine – north-west a turned ankle, a traffic accident, for after days in the open country, every bus seemed about to dispatch me to the next world. Fantasy went into overdrive as I imagined myself collapsing with a heart attack within yards of the cathedral. Once in the Westgate I calmed down a little, the milling tourists became modern pilgrims as I sought the calm of the Eastbridge Hospital, founded in 1180 as a lodging place for poor pilgrims. Eight hundred years later and its doors were still open; I could enter freely, and spent a few moments seeing where the medieval pilgrims would have slept and worshipped.

Through the Westgate, the last surviving gate of the original eight, and I was standing before the cathedral. I half closed my eyes and imagined how the pilgrim of the Middle Ages would have arrived:

> The pilgrim was greeted at his destination by a scene of raucous tumult. On the feast day of the patron saint a noisy crowd gathered in front of the church. Pilgrims mingled with jugglers and conjurers, souvenir sellers and pickpockets. Hawkers shouted their wares and rickety food stalls were surrounded by mobs of hungry travellers. Pilgrims hobbling on crutches or carried on stretchers tried to force their way through the crush at the steps of the church. Cries of panic were drowned by bursts of

hysterical laughter from nearby taverns, while beggars played on horns, zithers and tambourines.[6]

This passage reminded me of the hawkers and beggars, the sick, the poor and the maimed, thronging noisily and excitedly around Indian temples, like Sri Chamundeswari near Mysore. But the confusion round the cathedral on this twentieth-century day in the middle of May had a very different cause. It was created by building and repair work, the great West Door covered with scaffolding and firmly closed. I had been told about this, but had quite forgotten and was disappointed that my first view of the cathedral should not be the magnificent nave. I followed the signs directing visitors and pilgrims round the cloisters, and suddenly a new excitement gripped me. The silver lining round the cloud of frustration caused by the building work was, surely, that I would enter as Becket had on the fateful day of his martyrdom, by the north-west transept.

Becket was walking with me as I followed the directions this way and that, passing an old man being helped down the steps by a St John's Ambulance man – 'It's all right, I can manage', the professional kept assuring the old man's anxious wife. Through the cloisters and I was there, not, as I had hoped, by St Thomas's shrine, but in the Jesus Chapel. My disappointment that I had not, after all, been walking in Becket's footsteps soon disappeared – I was in any case within yards of the shrine – and I lit a candle for John, confident that Thomas would not mind my preferring my husband over him, and sat down in one of the pews.

---

[6] Jonathan Sumption, *Pilgrimage: An Image of Mediaeval Religion* (Faber and Faber, 1975), p.300.

We had done it, we had walked 150 miles and we were there, in Thomas's cathedral, where he worshipped and celebrated Mass, very near the place where he was murdered and the site of the shrine where so many had come to pray to him and ask for his intervention in their lives. I felt closer to him, warmer towards him. (It seemed significant that at last, like a true Becket lover, I could refer to him as 'Thomas'.) Somehow he was present as a brave and stubborn man, standing up for his beliefs, and I could admire him, even love him, for his courage and doggedness. But could I revere him as a saint? At that moment it did not seem important. I felt a deep peace – not to mention considerable physical relief that the long days of walking were over – and a small sense of achievement. But my mind had slipped into neutral, overwhelmed by the significance that was there, somewhere, but unable to pull coherent thoughts out of the maze of emotions. The confluence of past and present, of the inner and the outer journeys, had met in this place, in this moment, and I could only sit, overwhelmed by the beauty that surrounded me.

The ancient beauty of the cathedral, the timeless chanting of the psalms, took me beyond thought. I could identify now with Richard Church, visiting the cathedral in the 1940s.

> My immediate desire, when I first saw the massive but featherweight pillars receding in perspective up the aisle, with their fellows along the nave crowding together through the angle from which I saw them, was to lift my arms likewise, and to seek a high place to add to my endeavour. I wanted to shout with the voice of an army of men entering somewhere in triumph. But of course I stood there, doltlike and dumb.

So I too sat 'doltlike and dumb', until the psalm ended and Canon Christopher Lewis[7] introduced the lesson by saying that 'Moses is telling the people of Israel that when they arrive in the Promised Land, they must not forget to be grateful to God and generous to others'. It did not matter that I had no great thoughts. For the moment gratitude was enough.

After Evensong we crossed the cathedral square to one of the elegant houses that surround the cathedral. Christopher and Rhona Lewis, whom I had known for some years, welcomed us most royally, toasting us in champagne and offering us tea, sandwiches, cakes and the warmest hospitality. They had also invited Canon Derek Ingram Hill and his wife. The Canon knows more about the cathedral than any living soul (he wrote his first guidebook when he was 11), so he was well able to answer our questions.

Eventually we left and drove back to Oxford. For much of the early part of the drive the road runs parallel with the Pilgrims' Way. It felt odd, speeding in the opposite direction, past the places that we had known so recently and explored at so leisurely a pace. The journey that had taken us nearly fourteen days to walk was over in less than three hours. Then home to a pile of post and messages and a broken washing machine. Life must now return to normal, but would it ever be quite the same again?

The memory of that fortnight was to stay with me for years. It is still with me now, over twenty years later. When we set off I had been filled with apprehension. It was not that I was expecting anything dreadful to happen outwardly, my anxiety was more over what would happen inwardly. Now my question was – when did our pilgrimage end?

Was it that luminous moment when we first saw Canterbury Cathedral from the top of the hill, dominating the surrounding

---

[7] Currently The Very Revd Christopher Lewis, Dean of Christ Church, Oxford.

countryside? Or when I reached the Eastbridge Hospital, a resting place for thousands of pilgrims? Or the moment when I stood in the cathedral precincts, barred from entering through the great West Door? We had set out to reach the shrine of Thomas à Becket, so the end should have been at one of the places associated with his martyrdom, but it had not seemed so. Nor did I have a feeling of finality as we heard Evensong, drank champagne with the Lewises, or even as I put my key in my own front door.

Had it been a significant milestone in the passage through the first years of bereavement? Certainly there had been tears and moments of sheer desperation and loss, but John had been with me all the way. I was no nearer to learning to live without him, but was I beginning to learn to enjoy his presence in a different way?

It was not until the next morning, when I went to Mass at Oxford's Benedictine College, Saint Benet's, that I had any sense of completion. Only then did I begin to realise how I had been changed. On the physical level, fitter than I had been for years, I was relaxed and comfortable in my body, able to stay still more easily than usual; in that way I had, I suppose, found a healing I had not consciously sought. Mentally I was more centred, less open to distractions, spiritually involved in the drama of the Mass as rarely before. The hours of trying, consciously, to live in the present had left their mark and I felt totally in the present moment, totally in that particular place – a conjunction of time and place that gave a new significance to the centre of the crucifix. There is no duality, not between dark and light, or God and humanity, or journey and arrival. All is one.

In the homily the priest spoke of the gospels giving us a paradigm, but reminded us that we each had to find our own way. This was eerily in tune with my mood. I was very conscious that there were many aspects of pilgrimage – saints, relics, shrines, for instance – that I had not been able to relate to as fully as the medieval pilgrims would all have done and as some Christians still do. Aware too that the places I had found most holy were not always the traditionally sacred centres of Christendom. Though concerned with our arrival and with its symbolic parallel, our ultimate destination, I had become more and more convinced that it was the journey itself that was the point. It was as the priest said: we had, each of us, both walked the same path and found our own individual ways.

I had been changed by this pilgrimage, but I do not expect to know how for a long time. Though on this Sunday morning I knew the pilgrimage had reached some sort of completion, it had not ended. This symbolic microcosm of the inner journey had to find its resonances with the longer, day-to-day, pilgrimage. Perhaps my inability to know when it ended was a precise reflection of its inner parallel. We were resuming our ordinary lives, our journeys of perpetual pilgrimage. This pilgrimage from Winchester to Canterbury had not ended on arrival any more than life ends with death. But I did feel that I understood a little better where the sacred place is to be found.

7

Nimmo – Shamanic Journeys

'I have been waiting for you for over fifty years.'

Making a pilgrimage is a wonderful balance of inner and outer journeying, somehow fused together to form an inseparable whole. Soon I was to make some very different journeys, in which I travelled only inwardly, but during which I had some experiences that I will never forget. They were Shamanic journeys.

Shamanism is the earliest known spiritual practice, originally a religious phenomenon of Siberia, Central Asia, the Americas and the Indo-European and Oceanic peoples. The shamanic journey is found in primitive peoples the world over, in surprisingly similar forms, even where cultures differ in other respects. There are shamans among the Navajo medicine people and Zulu healers, in Inuit, Celtic and Nepalese cultures as well as in much of Europe.

Mircea Eliade, the great historian of religion, celebrated the shaman as the truly religious man, and defined it as a technique for attaining ecstasy that enabled persons to come into contact with the sacred order of the cosmos. As tribal cultures gave way to 'civilisation' shamanism was disappearing, but the end of the twentieth century saw its renaissance, possibly owing something to the desire for direct experience that has become ever stronger among westerners disenchanted with formal religious structures.

At first sight it seems a bit far-fetched - that one should travel mentally and spiritually from our normal world, known in shamanism as the Middle World, to the Upper World, the home of teachers and ancestors, and the Lower World, where the seeker can meet power animals and spirit guides. And there too one meets these teachers and learns from their wisdom. A bit crazy? Another example of our weird contemporary spirituality? Not a bit of it, I am convinced. An American shaman who has practised since 1961 is confident of the validity of contemporary shamanism:

> these new practitioners are not 'playing Indian', but going to the same revelatory spiritual sources that tribal shamans have travelled to from time immemorial. They are not pretending to be shamans: if they get shamanic results for themselves and others in their work, they are indeed the real thing. Their experiences are genuine and, when described, are essentially interchangeable with the accounts of shamans from non-literate tribal cultures. The shamanic work is the same, the human mind, heart and body are the same; only the cultures are different.[1]

You don't go off on a journey into the unknown without a briefing from someone who has been there before, and I was lucky in having a sensitive westerner, living in Oxford, to introduce me to this ancient practice: someone to guide, witness and assess. Caitlin Matthews is not only an experienced shaman, who writes and lectures widely, but she is also a wise guide for those who want to embark on this spiritual adventure. I knew virtually nothing about shamanism and am indebted to her for guiding me through a dozen or so memorable journeys.

---

[1] Michael Harner, *Way of The Shaman* (HarperSanFrancisco, 1990), p.x .

I have never forgotten my first journey. I had no idea what was ahead. All I knew was that I could seek the answer to a carefully thought out and genuine question, but I barely knew what I wanted to ask.

Caitlin was sitting a few yards from me in the little hut in her garden that was to become the physical starting point for these excursions into the realms of the spirit. She explained how, in shamanic language, I was in the Middle World, the world I knew and where I had lived for my entire conscious life. The place where I had met such a variety of human desires and emotions; the place from which I had reached endlessly for their fulfilment. But while this Middle World is often tantalisingly out of touch with the source of our feelings and emotions, the shamanic journey would take me to other worlds. It would take me to the Lower World, where one goes to one's roots, the depths of the world: the world that some traditions think of as hell, but in shamanic thinking is a world which holds deep truths and is the realm of power. And to the Upper World, home of the great archetypes, the plans, the blueprints – the heaven of the western world. All worlds should be approached with awe, for we are never far from the face of God. And she emphasised that the key to moving around these worlds is love: all shamanic travel is rooted in love.

I knew she would not direct the path my journey took or in any way interfere with it – that was up to the forces of the spirit world and to my receptivity – a quality with which I am not abundantly graced. As with any journey into the unknown, my job was to be alert and to gather together any courage I could find. I must submit to the unconscious, to allow myself to be directed rather than to direct my course. I was reminded of the words of the Lebanese poet Kahlil Gibran: 'think not you can direct the course of love, for love, if it finds you worthy, directs your course.'[2]

Caitlin told me to lie on the divan bed, to put on dark glasses to shield my eyes and a microphone round my neck, so that I could record what happened on the journey. She then played various rhythms on a drum, asking me to choose which one appealed to me as the sound to take me into the other world and to call me back from it. My first journey would be to the Lower World, as that is the realm of power, the root of the tree of understanding. And my first task – if task is not too active a word for an essentially receptive quest – was to meet my 'power animal', the helping spirit that could be thought of as a 'guardian angel'. This was an entirely new concept to me, but she assured me that my power animal would guide and support me on my journey and is an essential part of shamanic practice. I would soon see why.

Immediately I panicked. What if I didn't find my power animal? I had always been last on these sort of occasions. I remember standing by the school gates at half-term, whichever parent I was expecting invariably the last to arrive: how as the other girls were joyfully collected and taken off for the day I would stand among the dwindling ranks of parentless girls. I was sure that, however hard I searched, my power animal would not be there – all my deepest insecurities were triggered by this demand. It loomed like an obligation rather than the privilege it was. Caitlin stressed that it was not a question of searching. You do not find your power animal; he or she finds you. And my power animal would be my friend, the best friend I had ever had.

She then told me what she called 'the first rule of divination' – 'if you don't want to know the answer, don't ask the question'. What she – wisely – didn't tell me at that point was that you

---

[2] *The Prophet,* Kahlil Gibran (Heinemann, 1926), p.12.

would get an answer and it would be so perceptive, so true, that if you didn't want to hear it you could be profoundly disturbed.

So the first thing I must do was to formulate my question. What was the real question behind my meanderings? Ten minutes of conversation revealed it clearly. Widowed and in my sixties, I wanted to know how to live my remaining years on earth without John, my husband. So one small individual found herself asking the question that has beguiled and tortured humankind since darkness was hidden by darkness and the first human being crawled tentatively into consciousness. Together we formulated my question: 'Please give me help and strength to find the purpose of my life.' She would sit with me throughout and at the end she would talk me through the significance of what had happened.

Finally she told me to think of a place from which I would like to start my journey, the place in this world that would lead me to the other worlds. That was easy. I have known the Scilly Islands all my life, loved them as the most beautiful place and knew in my heart that these small islands, surrounded by seas familiar with every mood, had given sanctuary to wisdom in all its forms and had moved in and out of the three worlds since time began.

I chose Bant's Carn, a neolithic Burial Chamber with an entrance passage and chamber, dating from some five thousand years ago. It is on a lonely, windswept part of St Mary's, surrounded by heather and thrift and just above the remains of an Iron Age village. It is higher than most of these low-lying islands, so you can see other islands stretching around you, it also has an easy entry into the tomb. It is surely an entirely appropriate first stage of a journey to the Lower World.

I say I chose it – in reality it chose me; it is the place from which I knew I would make my journey, the place to which I would always return.

I settle on the shaman's long comfortable couch, my eyes protected by black glasses. Soon the drum beat begins, mysterious, inexorable, rich with hidden meaning, a steady rock to cling to, an encouragement to adventure. The drum beats sound for a long time, insistent, comforting, expectant, taking me already far into the depths of something – though I do not yet know what. So I lie, rather apprehensively, wondering if I am going to venture into the unknown or whether my deep-rooted claustrophobia will stop me before I even start, whether I will have the courage to enter the tomb. Ah, I see it now. It's narrower than I remembered and I'm not even sure there is room for me to squeeze in. I'm not sure I want to. But curiosity is stronger than fear.

I leave my possessions behind – very out of character this, but I do not want to be encumbered. I try to go feet first and am not sure if I have got larger or the entrance has become smaller, but I cannot enter. Immediately I begin to feel exiled, unwanted – I cannot even get through the opening to start my journey. Then I realise. It is I who have got bigger, or rather I who have become very aware of my hips, my femininity – whether I have actually got larger or not is incidental, the point is that I am already being given a symbolic lesson – it is my femininity that is making this journey. I must learn to be receptive. But this is not a woman's tomb. My toes and legs are in, but my hips are stuck, I come out again and consider going in head first, but decide that is too frightening. I stand, wondering, and the tomb widens slightly. Instead of being coffin shaped it shows me a few steps down. I take one last look at the sunlight, one last look at the Island of Samson, resting quietly in the sea a few miles north west of Bant's Carn, and go down.

I am in a cave, with the drip, drip, drip of water. It's not frightening at all, not once I'm there. The cave is round and the walls are smooth. There is a way through somewhere – I know it, but I cannot yet see it. I stay still to get used to the darkness. I begin to see a little bit of light, enough to see some moss growing – it's very short and dense. Drops of water trickle gently from the rock. It's all right. I'm apprehensive, but curiosity is still winning over fear. I just wish there were more signs of life. Apart from the little bit of moss there's nothing alive, yet it doesn't feel dead and I am not really frightened; I think it's more that I expect to be, that I feel I should be frightened. In any case I know I can go back if I want to. I feel something is going to slide open and let me through, so I just keep waiting. I'm not going to search for an opening, it's going to reveal itself – I even know where. It will be just to the left of the moss, where the rock is a slightly paler shade of grey. And look, it's starting to open, almost asking me 'Is this wide enough for you?' And I have to say, 'Well, if you could open a little wider it would be easier for me.' Oh how the universe co-operates if you don't force it … it opens a little more – it even shows me a little light, glimmering far off, inextinguishable, confidence-giving … Even if I am venturing into the unknown, something – everything? – is on my side, helping me. The sounds of harmony are filtering into this deep, unknown cave and it would be very ungracious if I did not co-operate. The gap is now big enough for me to go through, if I crouch on all fours. I start crawling – word of babyhood, word of subservience – but it is neither, it is enquiring, purposeful.

I crawl on towards the light, the grey now streaked with yellow, as if it were catching rays of sunlight. The opening had seemed short and inviting, this second stage seems endless; I keep moving but don't seem to reach its end or even see any signs of an approaching end. I remember the wonderful advice I was given on how to cope with bereavement: 'Plod on', I was told. How true it was: all I could do then was plod on. 'Please help me to plod on now. But I'm tired of plodding. I want to arrive … keep going … keep going …'

Almost imperceptibly the view is getting wider. Somehow – it doesn't make sense in terms of actual place – I can see the sea and Samson in the distance, just as I had from the Middle World I had left behind me. It's as if the place I am in hasn't changed so much as my perception of it. My little corner of this newly perceived world is not uncomfortable, not harsh, unkind or rough – but it is lonely. There is no one there and I don't know what or who I am looking for. I remind myself that I am not looking for my power animal, or rather that he or she will find me. I'm coming out into a much bigger, lighter, cave and the yellow comes to dominate the grey; light is overcoming darkness. At last I see someone, a very small, brown-skinned man, sitting cross-legged in the corner. He's not at all interested in me, but at least he's a living presence. Could he be something to do with my power animal? Is it him playing the drums, that persistent, inviting, cajoling sound that beats through my body, through my whole being?

❧

It is his nose I see first. Soft, velvety, at least two shades of grey, a little white, with that strange elasticity and strength of a horse's nose. I could see it under the guy rope of the tent I am now in, grazing, in a slightly absent-minded way as if it's owner's mind were on something else, as if he were waiting for something, patiently. As if he had been waiting for so long that he had almost given up. As if he were bored and needed something to do. He couldn't just stand there any more, but nor could he leave. He had an appointment and he was loyal and reliable; he would not let down the person he was meeting. So he grazed...

I know immediately that this is who I have come to meet, but I can't believe I have met him so quickly. I am overcome, quite unable to speak, so I linger inside the tent, almost shyly, watching the tireless grazing, up and down, stop and chew, up and down ...whispers of steamy breath drifting under the guy ropes towards me – and I stand, imagining the noble head above the nose, the strong grey and white body I knew would be there, the fine mane, the lively springing tail of this supreme king of animals. I hesitate for a long time, for I know that this is my power animal; that once I reveal myself I will never again not be known, from the moment when I approach him my every secret will be shared. Almost worse – yet oh how exciting – he will know more about me than I know myself. I cling to my last moments of privacy. It is a turning point in my life, a gate to pass through as significant as any freemason's passing, as any soul knocking at St Peter's Gate.

I am silenced by joy, wordless, motionless, but at last I go outside the tent, to see the animal whose body I have so far only imagined, whose grazing nose had somehow told me so much. He looks up rather as one might stop doing the crossword when a late lunch companion eventually turns up. 'There you are,' he says, 'I have been waiting for you for fifty years.'

I had not searched – I had not had time to – and I had found, or rather I had been found. As soon as I had entered that strange and sacred realm where I was told I would find my guide, immediately there he was. I had met my power animal, my guide, my guardian spirit; the kindest, gentlest and most utterly reliable friend. This beautiful grazing horse, who said he had been waiting for me for fifty years. He had been waiting for me for half a century, so he must know me, but I didn't even recognise him … then it dawned on me. It was Nimmo, the horse of my childhood, the beloved stallion who grazed in a paddock in the Berkshire village a mile from where we lived and whom I used to visit compulsively. He was a yearling at the time, somebody told me. I had never heard the word and I remember thinking what a beautiful word it was, 'Year-ling … '. It was my dream to own this horse – as if such a horse could be 'owned', but there was no question of that so I just visited him, watching him over the fence, feeding him, needing him, most of all loving him. I had said to the Shaman that for some time I had been feeling that I was waiting, but didn't know what I was waiting for – could I have been waiting to meet my power animal? She said that yes, that could be so, but it was important to remember that you don't choose your power animal; it chooses you. Nimmo had remembered me, had come and chosen me and I rejoiced.

The shaman had said: 'Your power animal is going to be like your best friend, the best friend you will ever have.' Already I knew she was right.

🌿

I start walking towards Nimmo, the sea brighter than ever before, the view familiar, but the surroundings strange, with palm trees amongst the downland and grass. I pluck up my courage to ask the question the shaman told me to ask:

'Are you my power animal?'

'Of course I am,' Nimmo answers. 'How could you be so silly? I told you – I've been waiting for you for fifty years.'

I stroke his neck, a lightly mottled grey, feeling it firm and warm. 'Are you Nimmo?'

'Of course I'm Nimmo. You're so slow. Where have you been all this time?'

Then the second question I knew I must ask:

'Will you give me the help and the strength to find the purpose of my life?' Nimmo says nothing, just nibbles my forehead, a sort of kiss. He looks at me with the most complete attention and invites me to ride on his back. It's a long time since I've ridden a horse and Nimmo doesn't have a saddle or a bridle – I'm quite scared. He lowers himself like a camel to make it easier for me to mount. So I do. How could I spurn an offer so lovingly given?

He gets up gently and starts walking very slowly … so gently, so carefully, that I am moved to tears, my whole body sobbing in relief at finding such a friend. He walks to a higher point of downland and stops by a palm tree facing Samson. 'We've got a lot to talk about, you and me.' 'Yes,' I say, 'and I don't even know the questions to ask. You'll have to help me.' 'I will help you.'

The drum beat changes, the sign that Caitlin had told me was the signal for me to go back to the Middle World.

'Will you take me back to the world I came from?' 'Of course I will. It's what I've been waiting to do.'

We start walking and soon I am back at Bant's Carn, with Nimmo, my power animal.

Nimmo introduced me to many wonderful teachers on these journeys – the Buddha, Nataraja – the Hindu God Shiva depicted as the Lord of the Dance, Jesus, who seemed to be a good friend of his, many angelic figures, a wise snake … and someone I at first called 'Little Brown-skinned Man' as I didn't know who he was. I had seen him on that first journey, just before I met Nimmo, and he appeared regularly in my journeys. He seemed like a sort of guardian, though I was not sure who or what he was guarding. He never noticed me and I became so absorbed in Nimmo that I forgot him. The second time I saw him he was holding something that looked like a violin. This time he looked at me briefly, but again he was not interested in me.

The third time I saw him was after Nimmo had been reprimanding me for always wanting to go somewhere. 'Why can't you just wait here?' he said. I did, and I was rewarded by the appearance of the little brown-skinned musician. This time I felt I must talk to him.

Shirley: 'What's your name, Little Brown Figure?'

Little Brown Figure: 'Why do you want to know my name?'

S: 'I think it would be more respectful to give you a name, better than just calling you 'Little Brown Figure'.

LBF: 'If you don't know my name, I don't think I am going to tell you. You ought to know. But I have got a lot to do with music.'

S: 'Are you my soul?'

LBF: 'Sort of – I am part of your soul.'

S: (excitedly) 'You're the Guardian aren't you? You're the Guardian, you are always quite near Jesus. You're guarding the way to Jesus. Are you one of my teachers? Can I think of you as my Guardian Musician?

LBF – now GM – Guardian Musician: 'I'm a sort of spare teacher. If ever there was a time when Jesus was too busy for you, or he had gone away or anything, I'd have a go at helping you. Why don't you sit down and we'll meditate together. Nimmo likes to meditate too.'

So here we are – a strange trio, my Guardian Musician, who is part of my soul; Nimmo, my wonderful power animal - and me. In what seems far too short a time the drums are summoning me back to the Middle World, but I ask my Guardian Musician if I can come again and talk to him. He says, 'Of course. Each time you've come I have been sitting here waiting for you. So please come back another time.' We say goodbye.

Soon, on another journey, I meet him again. It seemed that Nimmo and I were going to a party, but Little Brown Figure was guarding the way to it – he wouldn't let me through. He was roaring with laughter and admitted he had been lying in wait for me. At last I am going to get a chance to talk to him properly.

❧

He takes me over to the fire and starts playing on his violin, which turns into a one-stringed fiddle. It's so beautiful I am lulled to sleep. 'No more words. Just be. Just let the music speak to you.' Who says that? Guardian Musician or me? I don't know and it doesn't really matter. He's becoming bigger, filling out and becoming more and more good looking, as if the music had completed him.

He apologised. 'I don't know why I started playing. I know you've come to talk. I just needed the music so badly. Did you enjoy it?'

'I loved it. But I'm frightened of music. It hurts so much. It's so beautiful'

GM: 'I know. I think you have got to try and stop being hurt by music. You do get a bit infantile sometimes when you listen to music.'

S: 'I know.'

GM: 'That's why I am your guardian. I'm a sort of prep school teacher. It's my job to help you with things like that before you meet the real experts. And that's your first lesson today. Just let the music be. You're always quoting T . S. Eliot, 'Music heard so deeply that it is not heard at all, but you are the music, while the music lasts.' Pay attention to that yourself. Just be the music. I think that's the most important thing I can say about music. What do you think, Nimmo?'

Nimmo: 'Yes, I realize this. You must let the music be. Let everything be.'

S: 'But I have got to put words on the page. I can't just lie around'

They start laughing again.

GM: 'Yes, you've got to let your head work. But have your feet, your heart, your soul, firmly in that place of being.'

I am a bit shattered and ashamed as I thought I knew that. My Guardian Musician said that I probably did know it, but I keep forgetting to act on it.

They take me to the party and I am over-awed. We walk through a Norman door into a semi-circular room like a bee-hive tomb, but studded with windows. There's a lovely clear light. There is no division. No friction. Somehow I know that they are all one. Nataraja, the wise snake, the Buddha, angels, even negative qualities, which have somehow been included. Everyone is very still. As they enter, Nimmo and my Guardian Musician become very still too. Even I become still.

I realise. They are taking me to the still centre. That's the lesson. I have to go to the still centre before I can do anything, or write anything.

When we stop meditating we go and sit by a bonfire. Then the violin and the bow get up, by themselves, and start playing. All by themselves. Quite high in the air with no one holding the instrument or the bow. The violin is playing by itself. Nimmo and my Guardian Musician are not a bit surprised.

My Guardian Musician turns to me and says: 'When you are in the still centre it just happens.'

🌿

On the rare occasions when I have told anyone of these shamanic journeys I am asked many questions, receive many challenges. Have you made other journeys? You seem to have 'swallowed it whole' – should you not analyse the experience, treat it more academically? Surely you should evaluate it, treat it more objectively? What difference has it made to your life?

How do I answer these questions? Yes, I have made other journeys, asked other questions and, yes, they have shone light on my life and brought a richness, a stillness, that alas is so easily buried in activity. But I do not seek academic justification. I know that what happened on these journeys has real significance. I do not need to check it with my left brain for I know that what I learnt is true.

These shamanic journeys have been – and who knows there may one day be more – strange and powerful experiences in my life. In my ordinary waking life Nimmo is always beside me, though to my shame I often forget him. I know he is there, patient and loving; that he will guide me and help me again. Meeting Nimmo and the Guardian Musician have changed me at a deep level I cannot doubt and see no need to challenge.

As much as the gentle wisdom of Nimmo, the extraordinary experience of hearing the violin and the bow playing by themselves, without a violinist to guide them, remains with me. It is one of the most powerful images I have ever encountered, the messages from it echoing to the depths of my being. But the theme is the same. Find the still centre and let go, get yourself out of the way, let the violin play by itself, don't interfere … A new set of commandments appears before me: most of all the need not only to find the still centre, but to realise that, once there, there is nowhere that you would rather be, that this is the place to stay, always, whatever activity you might be involved with. If one could live the message of this image, follow these subtly given suggestions, the ego might take its place as a power occasionally needed, but more often giving way to acceptance, grace, gentleness. And most of all one might learn to accept one's own nothingness and so take one's rightful place in the oneness to which we all belong.

I still have not learnt, still have so much to learn, but this image, together with other journeys into the Lower and Upper Worlds of shamanic wisdom, have changed me like my first visit to Greece changed me, like falling in love, like meditation or beautiful liturgy, like bereavement, like going on pilgrimage, like hearing Mozart or looking at the work of Chagall. For better or worse, they are part of what I now am and I am grateful beyond words.

8

A Month in India – Discovering Interfaith

'God is one but his names are many.'

The pilgrimage to Canterbury and the shamanic journeying helped me to live again. Though with John's death part of me had gone for ever, there were other parts that were knocking at the door, wanting space and attention. Perhaps the strongest was the yearning for eastern spirituality, springing mostly from an instinctive attraction, but also coupled with a conviction that however deeply one believes in Christianity, it cannot be the only way; no religion should deny the truth held by other religions.

John had never discouraged me from pursuing this interest and I am not sure why, during the years of our marriage, I let my interest sit on the back burner and turned the heat so low it was barely simmering. Perhaps it was simply that I was so immersed in this new Catholic life, so occupied by the numerous Catholic activities and people that were part of this life, that there was little time or energy to wander further afield.

I should add that while interfaith did not much interest John, ecumenism did. He cared deeply about the relationship between Christians of different denominations and I was intensely moved by his reaction to a meeting between Archbishop Runcie and Pope John Paul II. In 1982 the head of the Anglican Church welcomed the head of the Roman Catholics and, with a dramatic gesture of goodwill, the two men publicly knelt together in prayer. Many people were profoundly affected by this and I always remember the way John summed up his reaction by saying: 'Now I can feel properly British and properly Catholic.'

I, however, was neither properly Catholic nor properly Anglican nor properly anything else. I was a melting pot of unformed beliefs in which ideas I came across and phrases I read resonated, moving me at a mysterious depth about which I was mostly inarticulate. They came from many sources yet they seemed to speak of one thing, and it was ultimately the same thing – that was my only certainty – though I was hard pressed to find a word for that one thing. The obvious word was God, but it has become inadequate through overuse. It also carries overtones of dutiful piety that do not bear much relation to the phrase brought into general use by Rudolf Otto[1] and which meant far more to me, the *'mysterium tremendum et fascinans'*, the fearful and fascinating mystery. Or perhaps what I really meant was something simpler to understand, even if hard to achieve – unity, oneness.

In 1993, the year I began to draw my pension, my spiritual world opened up in most exciting ways. Barely three months after I returned home from the pilgrimage – which itself had opened doors through which I had glimpsed as yet untasted possibilities – I set out to spend a month of my new and unwanted freedom in India. I was one of a small group of people organised by Peter Spink, a wise and generous-hearted man who had been a missionary, served as Anglican chaplain to British embassies abroad, was a canon on the staff of Coventry Cathedral and, in 1980, founded the Omega Order, a modern ecumenical religious community which drew people from all over the world. Eventually, quietly, as he did not want to create confusion among his followers, by then numerous and worldwide, he became a Roman Catholic.

---

[1] Rudolf Otto, *The Idea of the Holy* (OUP, 1923).

Peter Spink was an eloquent spokesman for a spirituality that he was convinced was struggling to be born. Over the last thirty years I had come across many aspects of the alternative spirituality known as the 'New Age', but the vision of the Omega Order was different. It was formed as a modern religious order within the traditions of spirituality exemplified by St Benedict and St Francis, it honoured the great Christian festivals, but its distinguishing feature was its concern with what the Order called 'the larger Ecumenism', or 'unity at the level of a common spirituality.' It is astonishing how often ideas that are pervading one's thinking, almost at an unconscious level, suddenly find form. Unity at the level of a common spirituality – wasn't that just what I was, almost unconsciously, drawn to? And here it was, the central tenet of a group I chanced on, some time in 1988, in an advertisement in the weekly Catholic newspaper, *The Tablet*. I was excited by what I read, so as soon as I could I went to Somerset to visit the small group that were living in a seventeenth-century manor house near the village of Winford. I liked the atmosphere, its emphasis on mystical awareness and the lack of emphasis on doctrine, so when, two years after John's death, they invited me to join them on a trip to India, I accepted eagerly.

❦

We stayed in Bangalore, where we did the things tourists do - wandered round markets, bought fine silks for a few rupees and ate good food for even fewer. We were shocked beyond tears by the poverty, tried in vain to dodge beggars, were entranced by the temples at Mysore, heard new age gurus like the extraordinary Sai Baba talk and watched him produce Vibhuthi, holy ash, out of the air. We ended with a few days of sun and sea at Goa, where I bought a brass Tibetan singing bowl whose ring starts meditations in my home to this day. But the high point, the specific reason for our visit, was a conference called 'Visions of an Interfaith Future', known as Sarva-Dharma-Sammelana, or 'Religious people meeting together'.

An attempt to create a global dialogue of faiths had been made as long ago as 1893, when the city of Chicago hosted the World's Parliament of Religions and the famous Swami Vivekananda gave a speech that many consider marked the beginnings of western interest in Hinduism as a living philosophical tradition. It was not only a key moment in the history of interfaith awareness, but also seems to nod in the direction of feminism, for its opening line, 'Sisters and Brothers of America ... ', was greeted by the audience of 7000 with a three-minute standing ovation. It was hoped that the next parliament would be convened seven years later in India, the cradle of so many religions, and though that did not happen then, here we were, 600 delegates from over 30 countries and representing all the major religions, attending a four-day inter-faith conference in Bangalore. It was a good feeling to be standing, 100 years later, in the tradition of those seeking peaceful, productive relationships between religious faiths.

The opening ceremony set the scene. We sat outside, just a few minutes' walk from our hotel in Bangalore, under a great awning; behind the speakers the words Sarva-Dharma-Sammelana were written in roses on a backdrop of marigolds. A group of Sufi musicians was playing as we assembled; there were welcomes, greetings and prayers from many traditions – Hindu, Buddhist, Jain, Zoroastrian, Jewish, Christian, Muslim, Sikh, the indigenous spirituality of Costa Rica, Shintoism and Baha'i. The spirit was of respect and love. We came from many traditions, but we honoured one God.

There were three programmes, one of workshops, one of lectures and the third, which was the one I chose, of visits to shrines, temples and mosques. Every morning we gathered for devotions led by members of different faiths, always in an atmosphere of mutual respect; we were careful to cover our heads or take off our shoes when that was the custom of the faith in question, we did our best to join in prayers and chants, whether we were familiar with them or not, and, most important of all, we gave ourselves completely, without reservation, to the experience.

The main part of the day was spent meeting representatives of all the faiths to be found in and around Bangalore – and there are many. We meditated with Jains and learnt about their doctrine of Ahimsa – non-violence. We met Buddhists from the Maha Bodhi Society, who greeted us with 'So beautiful to see you, from so many religions. Like decorating a temple with different flowers'. We worshipped with Sikhs and listened to Muslims from the Arabic College. We visited one of Sri Aurobindo's ashrams and the Ramana Maharshi Centre; we spent some time in the mission founded in the name of Ramakrishna, whose followers use religious practices from Hindu, Christian, Muslim and Sikh traditions and whose most famous disciple was Vivekananda, the Indian sage whose words so electrified the delegates to Chicago 100 years before. Here we were reminded that Vivekananda used to say, 'My God, the poor; my God, the suffering; my God, the oppressed'. Christianity was beautifully represented by the Bangalore National Biblical Catechetical and Liturgical Centre,[2] who blend Christian liturgy with Indian music and symbolism. Never have I seen the Gospel more reverently honoured than by the blue-robed nuns, as they carried the flower-strewn Bible in a gently swaying, dancing procession. Everyone we met welcomed us, showed us round and was happy to answer our questions. Many of them entertained us most generously, notably the Sikhs, who

---

[2] N.B.C.L.C. is an all-India institution set up in Bangalore to promote and co-ordinate the renewal of Christian life in the Church according to the principles outlined by Vatican II Council.

fed everyone who had attended their service – there must have been at least five hundred of us sitting cross-legged as we were served with rice and dahl and vegetables from great steaming vats.

It was the most memorable, exciting and moving experience and my respect for these faiths was boundless. All instincts about the value and integrity of other religions were confirmed. But I was left with many questions. On the one hand I knew, more clearly than I had ever known before, that it is easier to aspire to a universal spirituality if one is firmly anchored in one's own tradition. Respect for other religions is not shown by blurring the edges of one's own, but by acknowledging the uniqueness of each revelation and the insights we can learn from each other. This time in India made me realise that all religions are both particular and universal – particular in dogma, doctrine and custom; universal in their ultimate aspirations and mystical dimensions. We need to find – and try to live – the universal truth contained in our own tradition.

On the other hand, I wondered how I could give myself wholeheartedly to a Christianity that insists that it alone is the full revelation of God, that wishes to make converts from other religions, even while claiming respect for them. It does not seem possible simultaneously to honour other religions, yet to put them in second place in a league table of faiths. I became increasingly confused as I wondered how I could call myself a Christian if that meant believing that my faith was 'better' than Hinduism, Buddhism or Islam. The Christian revelation has its own uniqueness – that God is in Christ – but that raises profound questions about how it relates to different cultures. How can a way be found to worship this Christ who said, 'I am the Way, the Truth and the Life. No man cometh to the Father except through me', while acknowledging the truth contained in other faiths?

'There are many ways up a mountain' was a phrase I heard many times during this conference. I came home longing for a spiritual climate in which we can rejoice in the God who is, for all of us, at the top of the mountain, yet rejoice also in the different paths we find ourselves on, as we struggle onwards. In talking to others I found so many people caught in the same dilemma, sharing in the same hopes, that I had unrealistic fantasies of the 'Decade of Evangelisation', which took place throughout the nineties, being followed by a 'Decade of Interfaith' to usher in the twenty-first century.

I knew that such unrealistic fantasies must be put away. I knew too that things were happening; interfaith was on the religious map – just. In 1965 the Vatican had published the declaration *Nostra Aetate* that affirmed their much-quoted belief that 'The Catholic Church rejects nothing that is true and holy in these religions.'[3] While this statement was of huge significance, many date the real beginning of the Churches' interest in interfaith dialogue to 1967, two years later, with the World Council of Churches Conference in Sri Lanka. Then the current attitudes to non-Christian religions were seriously challenged and this conference was considered to mark a new departure in the relationship between Christianity and other faiths.

The Christian Church was at the beginning of a long and difficult journey, which is still nowhere near its end. The desire for people of different faiths to live together, to understand each other, even sometimes to worship together, is fraught with problems. No religion wants its faith watered down by unthinking sharing with others, however well meant; all religions want to preserve their purity, their traditions and their organic

---

[3] *Nostra Aetate*, p. 63.

relationship to their source. Yet, from the Christian perspective, there are many who long for the Church to accept that there is a depth of wisdom in the East that can enrich our lives and bring us more deeply into our own faith. I was one of many who were discovering that the practice of eastern meditation and the reading of ancient texts like the Upanishads, written years before the Gospels, can help us to glimpse one blazing, transcendent truth – a truth beyond all religious division.

The Churches had started on that journey, but in the 1990s it was as if two tides were running in opposite directions. On the one hand interreligious dialogue flourished and countless individuals, including many Christians, practised meditations based on eastern traditions. In the company of these people it seemed that the doors were opening, that Christians were being encouraged to believe that the exploration of eastern spirituality, far from being forbidden territory, was approved. On the other hand the Church's generosity to other religions seemed to have ebbed since the *Nostra Aetate* pronouncement of 1965; now the newly opened doors were guarded with suspicion. For instance in 1989 there was a pronouncement from the Vatican, called provocatively 'Erroneous ways of praying', that warned of the dangers of fusing Christian meditation with that which is non-Christian. This was then softened by the assurance that these ways should not be rejected out of hand simply because they are not Christian. The pendulum swung back as methods of meditation from Hinduism and Buddhism, Zen sitting, Transcendental Meditation and Yoga were now described as 'a problem', though apparently the Vatican consulted no one in India and its letter presented a purely western view.

I knew there were many church-based initiatives starting up in Britain, that many priests and religious were responding to the religious diversity that was becoming a characteristic of the country, especially of its major cities. The Inter Faith Network was founded in 1987, chaired by a Christian priest, Dr Tom Butler, and a lecturer in Hindu studies, Dr Nawal Prinja; Oxford, where I live, has a lively Round Table of Religions. There are many others. But one group for which I have always had a special admiration is based in Southall, a microcosm of multi-faith Britain. There are in Southall Grenadans from the Caribbean, Malayalis, Tamils, Goans, Pakistanis, a sprinkling of Irish and more recently Poles and others from Eastern Europe. To meet their spiritual needs there are ten Sikh gurdwara temples, four mosques, three Hindu temples, a Buddhist vihara and many Christian churches. Predictably Southall has enormous social problems, but it is also one of the most vibrant and diverse communities in the country, over the years drawing students and seminarians from both Britain and overseas wanting to engage in dialogue, as well as Asians, eager to taste the lifestyle and drawn as much by the mosques and temples as by the colourful shops and restaurants.

It is here that a group of Jesuits started an interfaith centre, called the De Nobili Dialogue Centre after the seventeenth-century Italian Jesuit who went to India as a missionary, so eager to understand the Brahmin culture that he adopted their way of life himself. Its founder and its director for many years was Father Michael Barnes, who believes that what any religious tradition has to offer is a gift to others and not a barrier to separate oneself from them. The De Nobili group act on this belief, trying to understand other traditions by living among them, sharing and talking with them. For instance they celebrate Diwali, the Festival of Lights, with their Hindu neighbours, feasting together and setting off fireworks in the gardens of Hindus, Christians, Sikhs or non-believers.

It is wonderful work and a delicate path for Catholics to tread, for though the Second Vatican Council has been reappraising its relationships with other faiths, it will not go further than to say that the work of the spirit can be 'discerned' in the life of devout Buddhists, Muslims and Hindus. This is subtly different from saying, as some would wish to claim – and I would include myself - that Buddhism, Islam and Hinduism are the work of the spirit.

Putting one's hopes onto others, whether brave initiatives in Southall or great institutions, is never satisfactory, never enough; the way to change is paved as much by individual action as by corporate rulings – women would have taken far longer to get the vote if it had not been for the actions of individual suffragettes. So as we left Bangalore and returned to our own little worlds, what could we as individuals do? How could we contribute to changing attitudes in other faiths? How could we help to speed up the movement towards tolerance and unity?

As is so often the case, when the time is right, things happen. I returned to England wondering what I could do to further this cause that reflected so much that was important to me, and there, amongst the pile of post that had accumulated in my absence, was an invitation to an interfaith meeting. I went along eagerly, only to meet my first disappointment. It was in a large bare hall, there were no flowers, no music, few visible signs of people of other faiths and all we had was a long, academic talk followed by a few questions. It might have been intellectually excellent, but it was so far from the colourful joining of minds and hearts and spirit that we had witnessed at Bangalore that I could not feel that this was meeting the needs of which I had become so aware. I needed to discover what, for me and for many like me, was at the heart of the problems we so often have in relationship with other faiths.

To do this I had to follow an instinct, which, I was later to discover, had good intellectual roots. For some time it had been becoming increasingly clear to me that the main differences between people's religious beliefs are not only between religions, but inside each religion. It is possible to be a Christian of a fundamentalist persuasion, with a strong adherence to biblical texts, or to be drawn more to Christianity's mystical expression in the writings of such as Meister Eckhart or St John of the Cross. It is possible to be a fundamentalist Muslim, even to the extent of the Islamists, who lean towards politics rather than prayer, or to be a Sufi, widely regarded as the mystical branch of Islam. The same gradations can be found in Buddhism, Hinduism – indeed in every religion. But there is a meeting point at the heart of all religions and that is, of course, the transcendent point, the top of the mountain.

Many years later I came across this expressed by the great authority on world religions, Huston Smith, and quoted by Frithjof Schuon. He writes:

> The fundamental distinction is not between religions; it is not, so to speak, a line that, reappearing, divides religion's great historical manifestations vertically, Hindus from Buddhists from Christians from Muslims, and so on. The dividing line is horizontal and occurs but once, cutting across the historical religions. Above the line lies esoterism, below it exoterism.[4] [5]

He goes on to explain that religions 'are alike at heart or in essence ("esoterically") while differing in form ("exoterically").' Later in the book Schuon himself emphasises the profoundly different natures of the exoteric and esoteric worlds, showing

---

[4] Quoted in Frithjof Schuon, *The Transcendent Unity of Religions* (A Quest book, 1984), p. xii.

[5] Esoteric – inner, mysterious. Exoteric – external.

that 'whenever there is incompatibility between them it can only spring from the first and never from the second, which is superior to forms and therefore beyond all oppositions.' He then quotes a saying from Sufism that illustrates, he says, 'as clearly and concisely as possible the different viewpoints of the two great ways: 'The exoteric way: I and Thou. The esoteric way: I am Thou and Thou art I. Esoteric knowledge: neither I nor Thou, Him.'[6] It was about dualism and non-dualism. Or in Hinduism, Advaita and Dvaita.

The Benedictine Bede Griffiths, who spent many years in India, had a simple way of expressing this. He would hold up one hand and, with a finger from his other hand point to the thumb and each finger - Islam, Buddhism, Christianity, Hinduism - Taoism - he must have wished he had more fingers at this point - then draw his finger into the palm of his hand, pointing out that though there were five different digits they all meet in the middle of the hand, just as all religions meet in God.

❦

So what was the most direct way to God? It is, of course, meditation. So it seemed that the best thing my friends and I could do was to put renewed effort into the meditation group with which we were involved. We had been meeting for some time, each practising our own meditation and, at the end, taking turns to choose and read a text which we would then discuss over a drink. I kept a record of the texts we chose and looking back find they cover a wide range of sources while focussing on the transcendent point. They come from the Upanishads, from the Christian Bible, from Rumi, Zen, St Augustine, the Desert Fathers, Taoism, Tagore, the Tao Te Ching, Meister Eckhart, Wordsworth, Ramana Maharshi …

---

[6] Ibid. p.47.

Two held a special resonance for me. One from the eighteenth-century Christian William Law, who had such an influence on John Wesley. We read a passage on the Unity of Religions which ends:

> There is but one salvation for all mankind, and that is the life of God in the soul ... There isn't one for Jew, another for Christian, and a third for heathen. No, God is one, human nature is one, salvation is one, and the way to it is one: and that is the desire of the soul turned to God.[7]

The other comes from the Bangalore conference. I have never discovered who wrote it, but I was immediately drawn to its simplicity and directness:

> God is one, but his Names are many
> Reality is one, but its ways are many.
> Spirituality is one, but religions are many
> Humanity is one, but human beings are many.
>
> There cannot be one religion for the whole world
> Religions are like flowers of a beautiful garden
> Every flower has got its own individual beauty
> Adding to the total beauty of the garden.
>
> Enjoy the flower of your choice
> While enjoying the beauty of the garden,
> Let not your choice be thrust on others
> Not be a cause of coercion and conflict.

---

[7] *Selected Mystical Writings of William Law*, ed. Stephen Hobhouse (Rockliff, 1948), p.102.

It was because of this meditation group that I was forced to think again about my attitude to symbolism. In a fairly random way I have collected a few symbols from different religions and by 1993, after my visit to India, I had several Buddhas, from China, Japan and Thailand – one of which I am particularly fond is a small but astonishingly heavy brass Buddha that I found in Delhi; Hinduism is represented by a Nataraja, the dancing form of the God Shiva that I had bought in the market in Bangalore and Ganesha, the Elephant God, whose role as the Hindu God of success must be involved with his reputation for overcoming obstacles, which in turn must have something to do with the elephant's sheer size and weight. I have a bronze and resin triple spiral dating from the Stone Age; it is copied from New Grange in Ireland, and is sometimes seen as a symbol of the Christian Trinity as well as singing of Celtic roots. There are several crucifixes – one a replica of the St Cuthbert's Cross from Lindisfarne, another, with the figure of the dying Christ, had belonged to John. I treasure a small stone from Morocco, 380 million years old, that I had been given – it speaks of no specific religion but resonates timelessness; I also have some OM signs, and if I could only keep one symbol, it would be one of them. This visual representation of the sacred sound of Hinduism, which I learnt to chant in Bangalore, seems more than any other symbol to capture the unending, infinite, limitless qualities which, it seems to me, we long for. No one has put it better than the French Benedictine, Henri Le Saux, or Abhishiktananda, in a prose poem in which he talks of 'The OM which howls in the storm and moans in the gentle breeze':

The OM which our rishis heard resounding in their souls, when they descended to the greatest depths in themselves, deeper than their thoughts and deeper than all their desires, in the existential solitude of Being.[8]

---

[8] Abhishiktananda, *Ascent to the Depths of the Heart* (ISPCK), pp. 189-90.

I love these symbols, but found an unexpected problem. Where should I put them? Were they private, for me alone, or were they to be a part of my house, proclaimed to anyone who came? For some time I compromised by putting them in the relative privacy of my study, but when I decided not to have lodgers any more and turned one of the lodgers' rooms into a meditation room - what should I do? The natural place for them would now be in that place set aside for meditation, but something held me back. It took me several months, and the sanction of a priest friend, to put them in the meditation room and so open to anyone who came there, not just the regular group who were of the same mind as me anyway.

The reason for this tentative approach was, of course, because I was still not sufficiently confident of where I stood to let the world know that I held the symbols of all religious traditions sacred. I was – and still am – deeply ashamed of this reticence. But at last I gained confidence and now, having moved to a flat, the symbols are on the central table, in full view of all who come. I love them.

If they upset anyone, no one ever said as much to me, in fact I get the impression that my friends too feel nourished by them. In any case I was soon confident enough not to mind too much if anyone felt they were inappropriate. But one incident has to be recalled. A friend was visiting, we were amiably sitting chatting, when suddenly, looking at the symbols, she exploded in anger. She criticised me for my beliefs, the fact that I was not totally committed to one particular religion or one particular branch of any religion, the fact that I am drawn to eastern religions - she laid into me until my hands were shaking like aspen leaves and I was on the verge of tears. I cannot remember the details of what she said, but to say she was upset by the symbols would be an understatement. What is so interesting is that she is one of my few friends who claims to have no faith, no religious commitment, no particular interest in religion or spirituality. Such is the power of the symbol.

❧

As the years pass I find more and more that in being so drawn to what religions share, rather than how they differ, I am in good company. In 1965, nearly thirty years before the Bangalore conference, Thomas Merton had identified the central need in finding the common point, either between faiths or, as in this passage, from inside the divisions of Christianity:

> If I can unite in myself the thought and the devotion of Eastern and Western Christendom, the Greek and the Latin Fathers, the Russians with the Spanish mystics, I can prepare in myself the reunion of divided Christians. From that secret and unspoken unity in myself can eventually come a visible and manifest unity of all Christians … We must contain all divided worlds in ourselves and transcend them in Christ.[9]

Merton was thinking the same way about the relationship between Christians as Bede Griffiths, who had symbols from many religions in his hut in Shantivanam, was about all religions. In 1976 he wrote: 'I have to be a Hindu, a Buddhist, a Jain, a Parsee, a Sikh, a Muslim, and a Jew, as well as a Christian, if I am to know the Truth and find the point of reconciliation in all religion.'[10]

Those who value ecumenism and interfaith know that it is from the depths of our being that unity springs and that it is from the depths of our being that it must be fed. So there

---

[9] Thomas Merton, *Conjectures of a Guilty Bystander* (Burns and Oates, 1995), p.21.
[10] Bede Griffiths, *Return to the Centre* (Collins, 1976), p.71.

is no escape, no substitute for personal, individual effort and involvement. It is not enough to demand that institutions like the World Council of Churches and the Second Vatican Council take ecumenism and interfaith seriously – though thank goodness they do; it is useless to argue that any one religion or any particular branch of Christianity is truer than another, even in the unlikely event of such a judgement being correct, where does such a conclusion lead? Only by making peace in our own hearts have we any hope of increasing the level of peace throughout the world. It is in the quiet hours, meditating on one's own as much as in groups and gatherings, that the hope of a transcendent unity becomes realised.

I knew that this was the path for me. But I was also coming to appreciate the need for a particular way; to realise that the more firmly one was anchored in one religious tradition, the freer one was to rejoice in the faiths of others. I suspected that it is not enough to float freely in some uncommitted world and hope to share the experience of others from an outside position. It was a curious equation – that to be free to respect and love other religions one needed to be lovingly and confidently anchored in one's own. I had still not reached that point of commitment as a Christian. It was the religion of my birth, my upbringing and my marriage, but not yet of my heart.

9

Double Belonging – 'Many Religions, One God'

'O God, let me follow you wherever you may lead me.'[1]

There was no escaping it. However great my wish to be anchored in one religious tradition, it did not seem to be the way for me. The physical and spiritual explorations of the pilgrimage, followed by the encounter with so many faiths in India, deepened my conviction that I could not stand firmly in one religious tradition, even in the Christian religion into which I was born and educated and whose cultural traditions had informed most of my waking – and indeed my dreaming – moments. As I began to accept this and to look around me with curious apprehension, I realised that this was, by the end of the twentieth century, a common position. In its further outreaches where attraction and interest led to commitment and practice, it even had a name – double belonging.

The phrase 'double belonging' emerged from the American 'process theology' of the 1930s and, in its literal sense, means to belong simultaneously to two religions at once. Yet the phrase is capable of various levels of interpretation, and some degree of double belonging is so common a part of today's religious climate, that we cannot ignore it. There is a further category known as 'multiple religious belonging' where the same issues become even more complex.

---

[1] A Muslim's first prayer on becoming a Christian.

On one level, its mildest level, double belonging might simply mean dipping a toe into another religion and returning to one's own faith with some new insight. I remember the first time this happened to me and how grateful I was. It was in the early 1960s, when I had just started meditating, and I came across the word 'nirvana'. It seems odd now, when the word is so familiar that there is a pop group and a fan club with that name and probably several hundred restaurants and health clubs, but then it burst on my consciousness with a thrill of recognition. Somehow it was fresh and wonderful, yet as familiar as my breath. It has been understood and translated in various ways – the state of being free from suffering, the goal of life, the eradication of craving, a state of peace.

I first met the word 'nirvana' in its use by the Mahayana school of Buddhism where it means 'oneness with the Absolute'. Immediately St John's Gospel, which for years I had been especially drawn to, took on a new significance of mind-blowing dimensions. A fresh wind of understanding blew through me as I read again words that I had thought familiar: 'And you now therefore have sorrow: but I will see you again, and your heart shall rejoice, and your joy no man taketh from you.'[2] Of course – if I really reached a state of peace how could anyone possibly take it from me? It would be part of me. It would *be* me. You cannot take me from me. I glimpsed the meaning of 'May they all be one. Father, may they be one in us, as you are in me and I am in you, so that the world may believe it was you who sent me.'[3] To find words for this realisation was another matter, but something had broken through to me, some new perception. At a deep level I was changed.

❧

[2] John 16:22.
[3] John 17:21.

Many people today find themselves enriched beyond telling by the rituals, symbols and thoughts and, perhaps most of all, the sacred texts of other religions. It could hardly be otherwise, now that there is so much interaction between people of different nationalities – we wear each other's clothes, we eat each other's food, we visit each other's countries and we intermarry: how could we not take an interest in each other's religions?

In the West we have, however, become accustomed to belonging to one religion at a time. We may be attracted to another religion and rejoice in its symbols, but to belong to it involves the sort of commitment that, when it comes to the point, few of us are prepared to make. I was aware that when I first practised a ritual from another religion – for instance greeting someone with the hands joined and saying 'Namaste', [4] or honouring the symbol of another tradition by putting an OM sign in a position where any visitor could see it, even when I was moved by a text, that I could not respond with the confidence and habit that I would in reacting to more familiar practices. I found, almost involuntarily, that I was asking myself how it fitted in with the Christian tradition which, whether I like it or not, is deep in my bones. Now that I have been following these practices for some time I am less self-conscious, recognising the significance of such symbols, marking their own relationship to the oneness to which we all belong.

This attraction to another faith can be a stepping stone to 'multiple religious belonging'. I read an article on that subject in a theological journal which starts with an American college student responding to a question about her religious identity. She said she was: 'Methodist, Taoist, Native American, Quaker,

---

[4] 'The Spirit within me salutes the Spirit in you.'

Russian Orthodox, and Jew.'[5]   I know many people who might
have answered in a similar fashion. However, this same article
goes on to refer to multiple religious belonging as:

> a contemporary, postmodern form of syncretism in which
> a person looks upon various religions as a supermarket
> from which, like a consumer, one selects at one's discretion
> and pleasure whatever myth and doctrine, ethical practice
> and ritual, and meditation and healing technique that
> best suit the temperament and needs of one's body and
> mind, without regard to their truth values and mutual
> compatibilities.[6]

I found the uncompromising disapproval of this statement,
from a journal published by American Jesuits, rather startling.
My confusion mounted with the words of a distinguished Indian
professor of theology. He was even stronger in his criticism of
some people drawn to other religions; in fact he quite simply
rules them out of his thinking:

> I would like to exclude a superficial approach which looks
> on the religious world as a supermarket in which one goes
> round picking up the best methods and elements that one
> finds useful for one's own purposes. I would also exclude
> people who claim to use the symbols of different religious
> traditions, freely moving from one to another. This is
> syncretism. These people do not know what religion
> means. Probably they are not rooted in any religion. They
> treat symbols as discarnate shells that can be filled with any
> meaning which one wants. They move from guru to guru,
> from cult to cult, from practice to practice. With such an

---

[5]   Peter C. Phan, *Theological Studies* 1 September 2003.
[6]   Ibid.

attitude they will not find anything permanently satisfying anywhere. Anyway, I am not talking about them.[7]

This statement seems a bit harsh on the numerous people who find themselves, whether they chose it or not, in this position. However Michael Amaladoss, the writer of this article and also a Jesuit, does later acknowledge that there are people who seek to experience other traditions seriously 'without seeking to integrate them too quickly, but living rather in tension.'[8]

❧

I hope he would have included people like me in this group, for I cannot deny that I am drawn inexorably to the wisdom of other religions, I am helpless in the pull towards an early stage of double, or even multiple, belonging. Nor do I see any reason to resist it, even though conventional bits of me, the bits that long to be safe, sometimes beckon, urging me to stay with the familiar. Perhaps it would be good to be whole heartedly committed to Christianity – apart from anything else it would be so much simpler. Yet rarely does a day pass when I am not surprised and delighted by some shaft of light shed by the teaching of another faith. From Taoism, for instance: 'Tao can be talked about, but not the eternal Tao. Names can be named, but not the eternal name.' Or this, from the great book of Hinduism, the Upanishads: 'He moves and he moves not. He is far and he is near. He is within all, and he is outside all. Who sees all beings in his own Self, and his own Self in all beings, loses all fear.'[9]   It is astonishing the effect of that last

---

[7]   Michael Amaladoss SJ, 'Double Religious Belonging and Liminality: an anthropological reflection' (*Vidyajyoti, Journal of Theological Reflection*), January 2002.

[8]   Ibid.

[9]   Isa Upanishad, tr. Mascaro (Penguin, 1965), p.49.

line, giving solace when anxiety becomes too much to bear. I love the Hindu scriptures, but I am not a Hindu. I am attracted to meditation in almost any tradition. I love the mystical texts of all religions. The die is cast - as Prince Charles said of his love for Camilla, 'It is non-negotiable.' I cannot cease to be drawn to aspects of other religious traditions any more than I can change the colour of my skin.

It is like being in a flower garden, catching delicious scents of roses and lilies floating through the air. Sometimes it feeds directly into one's own faith, deepening and enriching it. Sometimes it simply takes one closer - to what? Does it matter what name we use? God, Allah, Tao, Brahman … Whatever is meant by those great words, some of them so ancient their origins are unknown, the insights of another faith can feed the soul and bring a contentment beyond expression. Christianity calls it 'the peace of God, which passeth all understanding.'[10]

Nevertheless I sometimes wonder if I have to accuse myself of 'picking and mixing'? Or that even harsher phrase, 'supermarket spirituality'? I have anguished over this question. Is it wrong that my big Lindisfarne crucifix lies on the same table as three Buddhas, the dancing Nataraj and the OM sign? That a picture of the White Tara of Tibetan Buddhism hangs in my study? That I treasure a leaf of a Bodhi tree, a direct descendant of the tree under which the Buddha received enlightenment? Am I 'picking and mixing' when I read the Upanishads, the works of Rumi, the Tao Te Ching? Is it offensive to practice arati after meditation?

In fact arati, the waving of lights before the deities in a spirit of gratitude, is a good example of the way traditions spread through the faiths. It is not exclusive to Hinduism. A devout Hindu was deeply impressed to find something very similar being practised for long hours in the early morning

---

10   Philippians 4:7.

by the Orthodox monks on Mount Athos. He referred to it as mangala arati.[11] I have seen a similar ritual practised by Jews at the start of the evening meal on the Sabbath. And I have heard that Ashkenazi Jews light candles, waving the hand around the candle three times, covering their eyes and reciting a blessing.

Again, many western groups these days chant the word OM or AUM, the sacred word of Hinduism, which is also found in Jainism, Sikhism and Buddhism. It became Amen for the Jews, and in turn it became incorporated into Christianity. Did these practices and these words have a common origin or did they spread by one religion copying the practice of another? And does it matter? Does the sharing of a tradition dishonour the practice?

Many years later this longing for 'oneness', the oneness at the heart of all religions, found an outlet in my own life and a new way of looking at double belonging. For a while I had somehow let my regular practice of meditation slip away, but in 1994 I started practising Zen, under the guidance of Sister Elaine MacInnes, one of the few accredited Zen teachers at the time and one of only two Zen teachers to be invested as *roshi*, (which literally means 'old teacher') to be also a practising Roman Catholic. I was immediately drawn to it and, with a break at the turn of the century, have practised Zen ever since.

Was this my own personal venture into double belonging? I practised Zen twice a day, I went to Zen retreats, I also went to Mass on Sundays. I considered myself a Christian who practised Zen. Many of us in our group were doing this and there was no problem at all, though one Jewish practitioner was upset by the

---

[11] 'Auspicious.'

cross that sits on the central, altar-like table. In fact being a 'Zen Christian' seems to bring nothing but good.

I turn to two Jesuit masters, examplars of those following this path. Robert Kennedy, who is a Zen teacher himself, feels that Zen Buddhism need not be looked at as a religion at all, but as a way that enhances any faith. He writes that his roshi told him 'he did not want to make me a Buddhist but rather he wanted to empty me in imitation of "Christ your Lord" who emptied himself, poured himself out, and clung to nothing.' He adds that 'This Buddhist might make a Christian of me yet!'[12]

William Johnston, an Irish Jesuit who lived in Tokyo and has written widely on Zen, said 'had I remained in my native Ireland instead of coming to the East, I might now be an intolerant and narrow-minded Papist hurling bricks and bottles at my Protestant adversaries in the cobbled streets of Belfast.'[13]

But most of all I was encouraged by my own experience. I could find no conflict between practising Zen and trying to be a Christian.

However, the exception does not prove the rule and there is no doubt that there are at least two sides to the question of double and multiple belonging. On the one hand the disapproval of distinguished and admirable Jesuits like Michael Amaladoss must be taken seriously, on the other hand there are voices like the great Mahatma Gandhi, who wrote that after long study and experience he had come to three conclusions:

1) All religions are true; 2) all religions have some error in them; 3) all religions are almost as dear to me as my own

---

[12] Robert E. Kennedy, *Zen Spirit, Christian Spirit: The Place of Zen in Christian Life* (Continuum, New York, 1995), p.14.

[13] William Johnston, *Christian Zen* (Harper and Row, 1971) p.2.

Hinduism. My veneration for other faiths is the same as for my own faith. Consequently, the thought of conversion is impossible ... our prayer for others ought never to be: 'God! Give them the light that thou hast given to me! But: Give them all the light and truth they need for their highest development![14]

Oh the relief in reading those lines! The great Gandhi supports my instinct to love aspects of all religions. It is not a question of 'if' I could do so, but 'how', for the way of double belonging is an intensely personal path. While there is plenty of opportunity to learn about other faiths, there are no classes in how to apply their truths to our own lives, our own thought; there is as yet no tradition of double or multiple belonging. However much we listen and study, in the end we have no choice but to trust our personal reactions and experience. This sometimes goes against the grain for those brought up in a tradition where the priest knows best, the rabbi is the teacher, the guru is the one who sheds light. But listen to the advice in this ancient Buddhist text, believed to come from the Buddha himself.

Do not believe in anything simply because you have heard it. Do not believe in traditions because they have been handed down for many generations. Do not believe anything because it is spoken and rumoured by many. Do not believe in anything because it is written in your religious books. Do not believe in anything merely on the authority of your teachers and elders. But after observation and analysis, when you find that anything agrees with reason and is conducive to the good and the benefit of one and all, then accept it and live up to it.[15]

---

[14] 'All Men are Brothers: Life and Thought of Mahatma Gandhi' as told in his own words (Paris, Unesco, 1958), p. 60.

[15] Kalama Sutra.

Once again the words of the great and the wise give me comfort; this passage gives those who lack it the great blessing of confidence in their own experience. I find it very bracing to be assured that what I believe is, in the end, up to me. Is this yet another way in which we should let the violin play by itself? That image from the Shamanic journey never leaves me for long – the violin, high in the air, the bow moving, the music thrilling into the air, but no human player to be seen. If only we could get our manipulative, controlling selves out of the way and let in the divine, the unexpected, the miraculous … then music would pour from us. And it would be 'Music heard so deeply that it is not heard at all, but you are the music while the music lasts.'[16]

So, armed with the thoughts of no less than Mahatma Ghandi and the Buddha, I at last begin to work this out for myself. I was finding more and more that it was not black and white, acceptance or rejection of double, or even multiple, belonging; it has to be considered at many levels.

At the most tangible level, the level that is so much part of my own life, of borrowing the signs and symbols of another religion. In other words my much-loved symbols of Buddhism, Hinduism and Christianity gathered together on the same table, proclaiming to me one truth. Or finding one's hands falling naturally into the Indian namaste greeting. Or in our Zen practice, regularly making full prostrations. Certainly this is picking and mixing, but surely it is not doing any harm, either to the symbol itself or the one who uses it? For me it is deeply enriching, deeply uniting.

---

[16] T. S. Eliot, *Four Quartets* (Faber and Faber, 1944).

On the other hand the writer and journalist Mark Vernon suggests that pick 'n' mix can keep one in a 'religious consumer mode', that it could prevent one from 'committing, preferring instead always to be choosing this or that or the other'. Then, he suggests, it could be 'hindering spiritual growth as much as it is helping.'[17] Given my love of symbols of different religions, I do not want to agree with this, yet I find myself unable to argue with it. It underlines the need for honesty in one's chosen path, for respect and care; it reminds one yet again, if one needs reminding, of the place of the mind in religion.

But all these differences can be reconciled at another level, beyond thought, beyond reason. They can be reconciled at the level of one truth, one God; at the level of mysticism, the ultimate religious experience that lies at the heart of all religions. 'God is one, but his names are many' the Indian poem has it. The philosopher Frithjof Schuon calls it 'The Transcendent Unity of Religions'.

This is captured in the words of all religions. The seventeenth-century Sikh leader Guru Gobind Singh, writes about God, who has no marks and symbols.

> He has no name, no dwelling place, no caste:
> He has no shape, or colour, or outer limits.....
> To the east or to the west,
> Look where you may,
> He pervades and prevails
> As Love and Affection.

Those who take the plunge and change their religion entirely will appreciate this Muslim's first prayer on becoming a Christian, from which this chapter draws its subtitle.

---

[17] Mark Vernon, email exchange with author, 7 February 2012.

O God, I am Mustafah the tailor and I work at the shop of Muhammad Ali. The whole day long I sit and pull the needle and thread through the cloth. O God, you are the needle and I am the thread. I am attached to you and I follow you. When the thread tries to slip away from the needle it becomes tangled and must be cut so that it can be put back in the right place. O God, let me follow you wherever you may lead me. For I am Mustafa the tailor, and I work at the shop of Muhammad Ali on the great square.

Mustafa would have had no problems with double belonging. He was able to let the violin play by itself. That powerful symbol was once again showing the way.

For me the problems of double belonging, the use of words, music and symbols that do not derive from one's own tradition, fade into nothingness compared to the dangers of what I call 'soft spirituality.' Spirituality is *not* just about looking at the sunset, though indeed spirituality might be there. It is *not* just about holding hands and baring one's soul, though spirituality might indeed be there too. The spiritual path is tough and dangerous. The Sufi poet Attar writes, 'Do you think it will be easy to arrive at a knowledge of spiritual things? It means no less than to die to everything.'[18] A famous Zen Master says, 'When you thoroughly practice *shikantaza*[19] you will *sweat* – even in the winter.'[20] And in Christian teaching we are told, 'Anyone who does not carry his cross and come after me cannot

---

[18] Attar, '*The Conference of the Birds*'.

[19] A form of Zen practice.

[20] *The Art of Just Sitting*, ed. John Daido Loori (Wisdom Publications, 2002).

be my disciple.'[21] Spirituality should never be regarded as a soft option.

Soft spirituality has become a greater danger today, as the loosening of traditional structures and patterns tends to dilute, flatten and universalize spiritual issues until they are the equivalent of the cowboy's long walk into the setting sun – beautiful, romantic, but ultimately spineless. Ken Wilber quotes a passage that nails this danger:

> We intend to explore a sensitive question, but one that needs to be addressed – the superficiality which pervades so much of the current spiritual exploration and discourse in the West, particularly in the United States. All too often, in the translation of the mystical traditions from the East (and elsewhere) into the American idiom, their profound depth is flattened out, their radical demand is diluted, and their potential for revolutionary transformation is squelched. How this occurs often seems to be subtle, since the words of the teachings are often the same. Yet through an apparent sleight of hand involving, perhaps, their context and therefore ultimately their meaning, the message of the greatest teachings often seems to become transmuted from the roar of the fire of liberation into something more closely resembling the soothing burble of a Californian hot tub. While there are exceptions, the radical implications of the greatest teachings are thereby lost. We wish to investigate this dilution of spirituality in the West, and inquire into its causes and consequences.[22]

One could argue that the way to approach this issue lies in the sincerity of the exploration, but that in itself savours of 'soft

---

[21] Luke 14:2.

[22] Ken Wilber, *One Taste, Daily Reflections on Integral Spirituality* (Shambhala Publications, 2000), p. 25.

spirituality', for how does one measure sincerity? We need to watch out for hazards as a mountain climber might watch out for a slippery rock. There is an emotional/intellectual scale that runs from a deeply intellectual approach, through a nice balance of head and heart, ending with a total reliance on experience in which the head plays little or no part. Those who despise the intellect and insist that the heart is the ultimate guide in all things can drift into sentimentality, find themselves unable to hear 'the roar of the fire of liberation', finding instead 'the soothing burble of a Californian hot tub'. Then there are others who, whether from some deep fear or some other reason beyond even their own understanding, rely on the intellect to the exclusion of the heart. And what is the point of anything if it excludes the heart?

Somehow the creeping dangers of soft spirituality are similar to the rocks hiding in the seas of double belonging. Both lead to the danger of forgetting that it is not the fallible individual who decides the great issues of life and death; not the fallible individual who arbitrates between right and wrong, good and evil. While personally I am in no doubt that there are serious dangers in 'the dilution of spirituality' referred to in Ken Wilber's quote, I am less convinced that there need be any harm in double belonging, provided it is approached with humility and reverence.

In fact the sense of belonging to more than one religious tradition is not new. An American theologian, Catherine Cornille, argues that religion in Europe, America, and Australia is just coming to terms with something that has long been prevalent in the rest of the world, particularly in the East:

The idea of belonging to only one religion has been more or less alien to the religious history of China and Japan, and in India and Nepal individuals visit shrines and temples and pray for blessings regardless of which religion a particular saint or temple might belong to. In the wider history of religion, multiple religious belonging may have been the rule rather than the exception, at least on a popular level.[23]

So I was relieved and excited to find this refreshing and balanced approach in the thinking of an academic who has made a special study of multiple religious belonging. The opening phrase of her introduction puts her position quite clearly:

In a world of seemingly unlimited choice in matters of religious identity and affiliation, the idea of belonging exclusively to one religious tradition or of drawing from only one set of spiritual, symbolic, or ritual resources is no longer self-evident.[24]

To my delight she asks why we should restrict ourselves to the symbols of one religious tradition when there is so much other food for the religious imagination. It is no longer, she continues, a question of which religion, but of how many religions one might belong to. I was rejoicing in the freedom offered by this way of thinking when she went even further:

This sense of conviction of belonging to more than one religious tradition is thus clearly growing, at least in the West. It may be argued that in this, religion in Europe, America and Australia is just coming to terms with a practice or a form of religiosity that has been prevalent for

---

[23] *Many Mansions? Multiple Religious Belonging and Christian Identity*, ed. Catherine Cornille (Orbis Books, 2002).

[24] Ibid. p.1.

ages in most of the rest of the world, and especially in the East.[25]

So multiple religious belonging is the rule rather than the exception and total commitment to one religion is, for most religions of the world, an ideal rather than a reality? This seemed to me explosive stuff. Who wants a theoretical ideal when the reality is so colourful, rich and God filled?

Cornille's position becomes even more realistic when she goes on to argue that there are degrees in understanding multiple religious belonging and that the way it is practised by some members of New Age religions is closer to 'a complete absence of religious belonging'.[26] This, she seems to be saying, is like idling in the hot tub of soft spirituality, which bears so little resemblance to the roaring fires of liberation.

It also rings true when she suggests that:

> The first and probably most common way of understanding and legitimating the phenomenon of multiple religious belonging consists of focusing on the ultimate religious experience that lies at the base of all traditions. [27]

Here is the nub. Here is an acceptance of the line from an Indian poem that strikes so simply to the heart of it – 'There are many ways up a mountain.' At the bottom of the mountain, and as we struggle upwards, it is often hard to reconcile theory and doctrine, we feel we are different from our cousins who call from minarets or who worship what to us are strange gods. But at the top of the mountain, if we ever get there, in the ultimate religious experience, or in the fleeting experiences with which

---

[25] Ibid. p.1.

[26] Ibid. p.3.

[27] Ibid. p.5.

we may be graced, there, surely, all is one. Once again experience is the only true criterion.

At the still point of the turning world. Neither flesh nor
    fleshless;
Neither from nor towards; at the still point, there the dance is,
But neither arrest nor movement. And do not call it fixity,
Where past and future are gathered. Neither movement from
    nor towards,
Neither ascent nor decline. Except for the point, the still point,
There would be no dance, and there is only the dance.[28]

It was becoming clear to me that gratefully learning from other traditions may be enriching, but that it is not an easy path to tread. So it is comforting to find that many, the depth of whose spirituality cannot be doubted, have been this way before us. There are even guides on this very contemporary path, though they are not, as far as I know, formally acknowledged as such.

There have been, for instance, numerous attempts to reconcile Christian and Buddhist thinking. The Christian – Buddhist dialogue officially began as long ago as 1896, as a direct result of the World Parliament of Religions, but the thinking did not spread to a wider public until the 1950s, with the publication of *Mysticism, Christian and Buddhist* by D.T. Suzuki.[29] This book first drew attention to the similarities between the mysticism of Meister Eckhart and Buddhism.[30] In the 1960s, the fresh winds let into the Catholic Church by the Second Vatican Council

---

[28] T.S Eliot, 'Burnt Norton', *Four Quartets* (Faber and Faber, 1943).

[29] No relation to the later Shunryu Suzuki of *Zen Mind, Beginner's Mind*.

[30] More recently the Dominican Brian Pierce takes a similar line in *We Walk the Path Together*, in which he writes of Thich Nhat Hanh and Meister Eckhart.

led to books such as *Zen Catholicism* by the Benedictine monk Dom Aelred Graham, widely regarded as a spiritual classic. The inscription in the front of this book is worth quoting. It reads:

> TO THOSE
> WHO WITH THE INSIGHT OF THE EAST
> SET IN THE GREAT TRADITION OF THE WEST
> MAY EVEN IN THIS PAINFUL WORLD
> BE HAPPY.

And that was half a century ago.

There are others such as the Jesuit William Johnston. I never forget the gratitude with which I read his *Silent Music*, published in 1974. He spoke for his time as few were doing then. The first chapter ends thus:

> If institutional religion has somehow failed those in search of meditation, this is partly because it has been unable to keep pace with the sudden evolutionary leap in consciousness that has characterized the last decade. We are now faced with a new man, a more mystical man, and it is on the mystical dimension of religions that we must fix our attention.[31]

People drawn to more than one faith are, in my experience, those who are drawn to the mystical dimension, for at the mystical point religions meet in a very similar, arguably even the same, place. And it is interesting how many of these writers of the late twentieth and early twenty-first century, so well in tune with their time, came from the Christian monastic orders. As early as the 1940s the extraordinary Trappist monk Thomas Merton had been drawn to the similarity between

---

[31] William Johnson, *Silent Music* (Collins, 1974), p.21.

the Christian tradition of silence before God and Buddhist meditation; between Buddhist emptiness (sunnyata) and the self-emptying of Christ (kenosis). The German-Japanese Jesuit Hugo Enomiya-Lasalle, who was certified as a Zen roshi in the 1960s, did much to encourage Christians to practise Zen. And many are drawn to the Vietnamese Buddhist Thich Nhat Hanh, who is so attracted to Christianity that he has images of both Buddha and Jesus in his hermitage and every time he lights incense, he touches both of them 'as my spiritual ancestors.'[32] There are other great writers and teachers, like the Benedictines Laurence Freeman and David Stendl-Rast, who acknowledge their gratitude to Buddhism without in any way regarding themselves as Buddhists and many Jews and Christians who follow Buddhist practices such as Zen, Vipassana and Tibetan traditions. In fact Jews who also follow a Buddhist path have their own word to describe their 'double – belongingness' – they call themselves 'JuBus'.

The outstanding figure in balancing Hinduism and Christianity is Raimon Panikkar, born of a Spanish (Catholic) mother and an Indian (Hindu) father. Enchantingly and inspiringly he says he is '100% Hindu and 100% Roman Catholic'. In fact he went further, famously described himself in these words: 'I "left" as a Christian, "found myself" as a Hindu, and I "return" as a Buddhist, without having ceased to be a Christian.'

Then there are people like Gandhi, who related easily to Jesus and the Gospels, but who never lost touch with his Hindu roots. And when I once asked an Indian Jesuit what his favourite spiritual text was, he replied instantly – the Upanishads. And of course there are the numerous people who practise eastern meditation techniques while firmly retaining their Christian identity. And who find no problems in doing so.

---

[32] *Living Buddha, Living Christ,* Thich Nhat Hanh (Rider, 1995), p.6.

I am beginning to think that, in my own life, I have been treading an overcautious line and that I should be bolder, more outspoken, in the attraction that the mystical paths of other religions have for me. Perhaps I have been too influenced by the outspoken disapproval of some theologians and by my own original fears of diluting one faith by enriching it with another. Perhaps I have taken too seriously the warnings I received early in life against leaving the religion of one's youth.

So we walk that fine line between learning from other faiths while trying to remain faithful to one's own. In the last resort, *'On est comme on est'* as my mother used to say. Or 'Here I am, I can no other' in Martin Luther's famous words. But I am still tossed in this sometimes stormy sea. I am enriched by other religions. I try to be a Christian.

I have a feeling, though, that I have nearly given up struggling. Perhaps at last I can allow myself to forget childhood indoctrination and to follow my instinctive drive towards that great unity, that oneness of all things that Traherne understood so well:

> You never enjoy the world aright, till the Sea itself floweth in your veins, till you are clothed with the heavens, and crowned with the stars: and perceive yourself to be the sole heir of the whole world, and more than so, because men are in it who are every one sole heirs as well as you. Till you can sing and rejoice and delight in God, as misers do in gold, and Kings in sceptres, you never enjoy the world.[33]

---

[33] Thomas Traherne, *Centuries of Meditation*, (The Shrine of Wisdom, Fintry, 2002), p.12.

One does not need to face this struggle on one's own. Apart from those around us and alive at this extraordinary time in the history of spirituality, there is a great company, a benevolent 'cloud of witnesses', whose life and thought consoles our confusion. For over thirty years, in fact since I left the BBC in 1979, I have been writing biographies of some of these figures. So the time seems to have come when I should explore that privileged and wonderful form of writing – the biography.

10

Biography – Another Sort of Immersion

My years as a biographer started, as the best things sometimes do, by accident. After 25 years working as a producer in the BBC, I felt it was time to leave. I had enjoyed myself greatly but I had, quite simply, done it for long enough. So one morning I handed in my notice and went, as usual, to my office. My loyal team were already there, secretary, assistant, researcher, assistant producers – there were about six of us. So I told them my news and waited for the exclamations of sorrow and disbelief. Not a word. Eventually I said, 'Well, someone might at least say they're sorry!' 'How can we?' said one of them, 'when you are sitting there with a great fat smile on your face!' They were right of course. The moment had come and though I had no idea what I would do next, I was happy.

One of the publishers I regularly came across in my work at the BBC had already planted the idea of writing biography in my mind, and I found my thoughts drifting in that direction. Biography is, I think, what one might call a midwife job and curiously, after I had been doing it for a few years, I realised how it fitted in with other things I had done – they were all what I think of as 'midwife' jobs. When I was a music student, a pianist, I most enjoyed accompanying other people, or as a viola player, playing in an orchestra. At the BBC I was first a music balancer – looking after the real musicians who were performing. I became a radio producer, where one not only looked for good subjects and interesting ways to approach them, you also relied heavily on your speakers – and much of the work in those days was helping speakers express themselves over the microphone. Then I was a television producer, where again one is a sort of midwife, holding a huge variety of people together, and attending at the birth of a programme.

Technically, compared to television production, biography is simple, for there is just you and your subject – and later on your editor. This means you have more freedom, but you also have more responsibility. Not only are you mostly alone, with no colleague with whom to discuss a problem, but you cannot, for instance, rely on your cameraman for beautiful pictures if your text gets boring; nor can you ask the sound recordist to produce some sonorous effects if your descriptive powers fail. And you certainly cannot blame anyone except yourself if you get your facts wrong. But again one is essentially a midwife – the interpreter of another person's life, the collector of views and information about them, the purveyor of their story to a larger public. Most crucially, you are the one who tries to present the essence of a person and of a life's work. It is quite a responsibility.

I find that writing biography is total immersion in another person. You have permission to be a detective, to enter the secret places of another life and to learn about every aspect of it. It is a wonderful, engrossing and fulfilling thing to do. The other day I came across a quote from the biographer Hilary Spurling, who put another side of any detective work. She said she had at different times been called 'scavenger, jackal, vampire, garbage-collector', then she adds wryly – 'all of them valid up to a point'. She is right, of course. Anyone who digs for treasure is going to find a shadow side as well.

Biography is in a way a second, hand creative art. You need to be creative but you are not – and should not be – the star. My admiration for novelists is unlimited. They have to create the story as well as write it, whereas the biographer has the story there for the finding. You are always the bridesmaid and never the bride – and if that role does not appeal to you, don't be a biographer!

❧

The choice of subject is of course crucial. I had no doubt where my biographical interest would lie – I knew I would want to continue the work I had been doing in broadcasting, to explore spirituality, particularly contemporary spirituality – the area that drew me so magnetically. It would not lead me to fame and fortune, but at some level I think I hoped to learn from my subjects, to deepen my own spiritual life through theirs. However, when I set out on this course I was so excited I had no thoughts of motivation at all. I just wanted to get going.

The starting gun was fired by a friend of mine who said, quite casually, why don't you write about Cicely Saunders? I had worked with this remarkable woman when I was in television and it seemed an excellent idea, so I went down to St Christopher's Hospice in Sydenham to ask her permission. She agreed – I was lucky in that no one had yet written about her at length - so I cut my biographical teeth on the doctor who revolutionised the care of the dying and founded the modern hospice movement; further, someone whose whole life and personality was lit up by her deep Christian faith.

I soon discovered that there are three main elements in any biography. The facts – and obviously they are crucial. The story, which in the case of Cicely was not only the story of twentieth-century palliative care, but also a quite extraordinary love story. Finally – and the strength of this last element surprised me – the relationship between writer and subject. And what surprised me even more is that the relationship is just as real, whether the subject is living or dead.

Research is hard work, involving travel, talking to people, hours of reading documents, diaries, letters and related books and – crucially – organising the sheer bulk of material you collect. Of course there is sometimes tedium, but there are many exciting moments. A tiny example. I was going through Cicely Saunders engagement diaries. She was an almoner – a social worker – at the time in question. There were several entries for a patient called David Tasma: just his name, written in the space allocated to Tuesday, 14 February 10.30am in her diary for 1947 - that sort of thing. I knew that he was the first of three Poles with whom she fell deeply in love, but I didn't know exactly when the relationship made that difficult move from the professional to the personal - and I don't think even she remembered exactly. Then suddenly the diary entry was just 'David.' It must have been then, almost exactly, that he became more than a patient to her. And when I reminded her of the entry and its date she confirmed that, indeed, it must have been then.

Then there is the question of access to papers and letters. I had a wonderful time when I was researching Desmond Tutu, because I was writing in the 1980s and his papers were not at the time even catalogued. So I was let loose in the University of Cape Town with piles and piles of paper in every sort of muddle. It was harder work, I suppose, sorting out the wheat from the chaff, but it was very exciting, never knowing what treasure you were going to come up with. Not to mention the joy of working within sight of both the Atlantic Ocean and of Table Mountain.

There are all sorts of dimensions to research. Studying the person's work – in my case this has meant spending one Christmas working in a hospice for Cicely; three visits to South Africa at the height of apartheid when writing about Desmond Tutu; for Teresa mostly reading her books and letters and going to Avila; for Bede and Abhishiktananda again much reading and spending time in France and India. And often it seems necessary to do some research in America, mainly to walk in the footsteps of your subject – Tutu, Bede Griffiths and

Cicely Saunders all travelled in the States. Sometimes you need to see people who knew or who had studied the person you were writing about, to find further papers, perhaps most of all to absorb the atmosphere and the effect that this amazing country has on people. It is surprising how much trouble one is prepared to go to in the quest for knowledge and insight about one's subject. I remember travelling for several hours each way to a remote part of Cornwall to talk to a friend of Cicely's. I think it only resulted in a couple of lines of text, but I did not for a minute resent the effort.

In the case of a living subject much of the main substance of the story comes through interviews – talking to the person themselves and also to their friends, family, admirers and critics. I interviewed at least a hundred people about Tutu, and I was deeply grateful to them, for as he was at the time Archbishop of Johannesburg and already a well-known public figure, he could not give me very much of his own time. I was surprised, in his case, at how little he seemed able to talk about himself. I remember asking him something slightly personal and he just laughed, and said, 'You know more about my innards than I do!' Perhaps that lack of introspection is one of his great qualities.

But most of all I love working with letters and diaries. They are primary material and usually precise about dates, so you know exactly when someone thought or did something; also people tend to write more freely than they do in books and articles, so letters are often intimate and revealing. And I suppose I have to admit to a small thrill at being licensed to do something that is normally off limits. To hold the very letter in which, many years ago, someone you have come to know intimately has tried to express the 'dearest deep down things' – well, to say it is a privilege is to put it mildly.

There are so many clues in letters apart, of course, from the actual information contained in them. The paper itself, especially if you are lucky enough to have access to handwritten letters, tells you something. The handwriting, too, even if you are not a handwriting expert there is always something to learn from the way a letter is presented. The style – do the letters sound like the person you are coming to know? I noticed that Bede Griffiths, whose life and thought took risks with his calling as a monastic, had three styles of letter writing. When he wrote to his Abbot and his religious superiors he was deferential and eager, for instance, to point out that the Vatican Council had sanctioned the inter-religious dialogue in which he was involved. When he wrote to his fellow monks and acquaintances he was a little more relaxed and open, but still guarded – he was years ahead of his time and his views could have caused trouble, might even have put an end to his work. But with close friends his real thoughts and feelings came out. I spent hours in the Bodleian, going through his lifelong correspondence with his close friend from Oxford days, Martyn Skinner. To him he admits – and remember he was a Benedictine monk: 'I am feeling very much the total inadequacy of Christianity to-day. Modern Roman Catholicism in the light of the Vatican Council appears as an extremely decadent religion, a kind of fossilisation of what had once been a great tradition.' He would never have written like that to his Abbot, but what a gift to a biographer, to have such a forthright view, complete with date – that letter was written as early as 1966 – and with further expansion of his thinking.

I haven't yet done a biography dependent on email correspondence and I would not like to do so. The feel of the paper, dated, with the address from which it was written, acquires a delicious, elusive significance. A bit like the power of relics I suppose – he or she, the one who is the centre of your working life, they *touched* this, they pondered over the lines as they wrote. They addressed it, in all probability they took it to the post box.

Sometimes there are glorious, mind-blowing surprises. Right at the end of the biography I finished in 2004 was a case in point. Abhishiktananda, a French Benedictine monk who spent the second half of his life in India, had some truly astonishing mystical experiences in the last months of his life, mostly in the company of another Frenchman, Marc, who is assumed dead, but who certainly cannot be found to talk to. I had covered these experiences as best I could through Abhishiktananda's own diary and through what he had said and written to other people, but there was no objective evidence and I had not really expected any. Then, by the most extraordinary stroke of good fortune, I found some excerpts from the most direct source one could imagine apart from Abhishiktananda himself – his friend Marc. I was lucky enough to come across some pages from Marc's diary and so was able to read of these mind-blowing experiences from the pen of the only other person who had been present and who was most intimately involved. It was like being the first woman on the moon – I couldn't believe my luck.

I once read – it was written by an experienced biographer though I can't now remember who – that a biographer should never use the word 'perhaps'. I disagree with this. A biography is not just a listing of verifiable facts, it is also drawing deductions from those facts, sometimes hazarding a guess at something that is not on record. This is particularly true if the subject is long dead and you cannot speak either to them or to people who knew them.

For instance, was Teresa of Avila in love with her friend Jeronima Gracian? Writing to him she was at her most impulsive and loving, their intimacy is indicated by the use of code names – she refers to herself as Angela or Laurencia and to him as Paul. She clearly enjoyed the conspiratorial dimension of their relationship, inevitable as she was a nun and he a priest. She was distraught if she did not hear from him, even envious if he stayed at other convents. Yet the popular conception is that it was John of the Cross, with whom she shared the most extraordinary mystical experiences, John of the Cross whom she loved. In this case I did not use the word 'perhaps', but the way I cover the two relationships – based entirely on what she herself wrote – makes it clear the conclusion I came to: the underlying 'perhaps'.

Sometimes one must hazard a guess and I cannot see that it is wrong either. A tiny example. Abhishiktananda was born Henri Le Saux, his parents running a grocery shop in Brittany. That is fact. One of the things they sold was coffee. That is fact. Henri sometimes helped in the shop. That also is fact. Henri came to live the life of an ascetic, so I suggest that, 'The background to Henri's later ascetism was a shop full of gastronomic delights – salamis hanging from the ceiling, bottles of wine and cognac on the shelves and, pervading everything, the aroma of good coffee.' Which is probability, not fact.

I have only twice knowingly withheld information. Once was when someone told me more than I thought was necessary about sexual matters. The other was a story I heard of someone's mild dishonesty. In both cases I came to the conclusion that neither bits of information added to the story or provided any insight into the person in question and I did not see the point in engaging in gossip. In a third case I was criticised by a few people for divulging something they felt I should not have done. I thought long and hard, discussed it with someone whose opinion I greatly respected, and decided it was a necessary bit of information. Such decisions pervade a biographer's life.

Research is at its most precarious when it involves people closely connected with your subject. Sometimes they long to talk about their revered friend or hated enemy, sometimes they are shy, unwilling, even frightened. I heard the other day of a book being written about a very strong character who aroused very controversial views in people. It turned out that everyone had been very flattering about this person – if not strictly truthful. They were too frightened of the person in question, and of each other, to be anything but flattering. Sometimes the truth is hard to unearth.

One important bit of research I will never forget involved creeping through a coconut grove one dark night in South India to see Russill, a very great friend of Bede's who was unwilling to speak to me about him, even unwilling to talk to me publicly at all. Yet he warmed to his subject and talked for two hours, all highly relevant to my work but all *off the record* – it was most tantalising. Would he ever talk to me on the record? He said he would think about it. I understood his problem. Though he was happily married, there had been rumours of an over-close relationship between him and Bede and he was not sure how to deal with them.

Eventually I went to America, where the person I most wanted to see was, of course, Russill.

Would he now talk to me freely? He and his wife welcomed me most warmly and, by the grace of God, I said the right thing. It was something like, 'You were really like a son to Bede, weren't you?' Their eyes filled with tears of relief – it was most moving. And then they both talked to me freely, even giving me copies of several of the extraordinary personal letters Bede wrote to them.

❧

I reckon to do about a year's research on a subject before I start writing, though at one level there is no reason ever to stop researching, there is always something more to learn. But the moment comes when I simply cannot take in any more information, when the urge for expression becomes overpowering, when, to be honest, I am bored of researching. Then I start writing, doing additional research as I go along.

So first there is the intriguing task of plotting, of arranging the bricks of my research into a story that is, first of all, true, and that has some sort of shape and form. To be aware of the peak moments, covering everything essential but avoiding being boring. One must never forget that biography is essentially a story – a *true* story. As a biographer you are going to be taken on a journey, a journey through someone else's life; and you, in a curious way, are in the driving seat, obviously not controlling how the story unfolds, but responsible for the way that it is told, the way it affects your readers. And you are not only writing about the person in question, but about their world, their time, their subject and clearly you need to have some knowledge of their special areas of interest; you can find yourself on exciting journeys. So looking back over the biographies I have written I am grateful for the various themes I had the chance to explore, the different stories I was privileged to share.

So it was straight into the deep end with death and dying, illness, courage and compassion as, at the end of the 1970s when Cicely Saunders was in her early sixties, I followed her extraordinary story from the death of her first great love along the path he, almost unwittingly, set her on. She became the leading figure in new ways of controlling pain, able to say, 'It is my experience in two terminal homes that we can relieve the suffering of ninety per cent of the patients and bring it within their diminishing compass where we cannot relieve it entirely.'[1] But from the outset her vision was spiritual as well as medical: 'Suffering is only intolerable when nobody cares and one continually sees that faith in God and his care is made infinitely easier by faith in someone who has shown kindness

---

[1] Shirley du Boulay, *Cicely Saunders: The Founder of the Modern Hospice Movement* from the Foreword by John Winton, Bishop of Winchester (Hodder and Stoughton, 1984), p.7.

and sympathy.'[2]   She was wonderful to work with, co-operative and non-judgemental.

Writing about Desmond Tutu took me to South Africa in the 1980s, where I saw for myself the unbelievable horrors of apartheid and the almost equally unbelievable courage and cheerfulness of the black South Africans: following Tutu's words and actions was again to see Christianity in practice. One of the things I learnt is how tragedy is more tolerable if you are doing something about it. I wept for apartheid before I started. I wept for apartheid when I had finished. But I didn't weep while I was there or while I was writing about it. The people of South Africa didn't weep, so how could I?

So my life in biography started with two twentieth-century people, both profoundly Christian, both living their Christianity in their work, one through care of the dying, the other through being a gallant fighter against apartheid. I am not quite sure why, in the late 1980s, I moved from the living to someone who died four hundred years ago; from Anglicanism to Roman Catholicism; and from Christianity in the world to the enclosed life of a Spanish Carmelite. That, however, is what happened. Sitting in the office of Hodder and Stoughton, talking with my editor about what my next book should be, I heard myself say, 'What about Teresa of Avila?'

I never regretted it. Though the cult of saints has never interested me very much, mysticism draws me magnetically and it was this longing I was responding to in choosing Teresa. And, of course, I found far more, because not only did Teresa have an extraordinary inner life but she was also a woman of quite startling courage, travelling round Spain founding Reformed Carmelite convents in the seventeenth century, before 'suffragette' was even a word. She did not, it's true, fit well into my continued interest in contemporary spirituality,

---

[2]   Ibid.

but figures as great as St Teresa defy category and time and I was not worried by any conflict: the common search was for the transcendent, whatever word is used. It was, though, a tough book to write, for it was while I was writing it that John's illness became really serious and writing took second place. I had continuously to say to myself, 'Teresa coped – and so must you.'

At this point I took a turning that I think any careers adviser would have warned against. Instead of seeking out leading figures whose biographies would be big sellers, I followed the mysterious instinct that had accompanied me from childhood on and had not been fully satisfied or gone away. For my next two biographies I headed east to follow the lives of two European Benedictines who spent most of their adult lives in India: Father Bede Griffiths and Swami Abhishiktananda, also known as Henri Le Saux. Neither were famous outside their own particular circles, both were exploring a new sort of spirituality, one that was in tune with our times and that was to have a powerful effect on an ever-increasing number of people.

With these two remarkable figures I could explore the thinking of two Christians who were open to the East, not as missionaries but as sharers and seekers, not as representatives of western Christian culture but as pioneers in a new understanding of spirituality. Most of all I could join them in their longing to transcend the opposites and find unity. Their influence was, and still is, so great in my life. They are very different people and their paths were correspondingly different, but more than any others they have transformed my understanding of the possibilities of bringing East and West together; of rejoicing in both similarities and differences.

One of the main reasons I love biography is that it's not only about story, it's about relationship – setting out to write a biography is to embark on one of the strangest relationships you can have. It's almost like a marriage, and when you finish the book and hand your child over to the publisher, it is almost like a bereavement. After finishing the biographies of both Bede and Abhishiktananda I was for quite a few weeks in a state that could only be called a depression. I had lost the focus of my working life, I had come to the end of a relationship. I sorely missed these figures who had been at the centre of my life for so long.

It is quite different to any other relationship you could have. It may be with someone you have never even met, but you have his or her life in your hands, as you inevitably influence the way in which your subject is remembered. Also, in a sense, he or she has *your* life in *their* hands, for they will cast a spell over your life – certainly for the time you are writing the book, possibly for ever. Undertaking to write someone's life is a big responsibility. It is also a risk, for your own life may never be quite the same again.

It was when writing about Bede Griffiths that I came across the extraordinary extent to which one can identify with one's subject. This is not something I would recommend, but it can happen, and in the case of Bede Griffiths, it did. I remember three occasions where I caught myself out in this identification. The first was at a party when somebody asked me how my book on Bede was going. I said – perhaps I should say 'I heard myself say' – 'Well, it's 1929 and I am just going up to Magdalen College, Oxford.' The personal pronoun and the present tense – what was I thinking of?   A few months later and a similar question – 'How is your book going?' I replied, 'Well, Bede has just set off for India and I have no material for the three weeks he is on board ship, so I suppose I can take a break.' The third example is mildly embarrassing, but here goes. I was visiting some very old friends of Bede's who had known him since he was quite young. For much of the time I felt that one of them, the wife of the couple, was trying to decide whether to tell me something, and I waited, curiously. But it was not until I was standing in their hall, car key in hand ready to go, that she said it – in a rather rushed and embarrassed way: 'Bede once told me that he had never been sexually attracted to a woman.'

Bless her for telling me. It confirmed what I had come to believe, nevertheless it took me by surprise and I was glad I was just leaving and could absorb this on my own. I sat in my car for a few minutes, and to my amazement my thought was, 'Oh dear. Bede would never have fancied me.'   How egocentric can a biographer get?

So the crucial first step in biography is choosing your subject. What do you have to think about here?   Even if you are not seeking fame and fortune in writing a biography, you have to be realistic about the commercial viability of the person towards whom you are leaning. If your publisher greets your idea with 'Who he?' or 'Who she?' you are not likely to get much further. Unless of course you are prepared to take a risk and just write it and see if the story is strong enough to attract a publisher.

Curiously enough publishers don't seem to mind if there are already other biographies written – even sometimes if they are going to be published at the same time. I have been asked to write biographies when it was known that someone else was already working on one. Apparently over fifty books and theses on Teresa of Avila have appeared in English since 2000 – ten a year - yet my own, first published in 1991, was reissued in 2004 and as I write in 2014 it is still in print. The message seems to be that a great subject has more facets than a diamond.

But there is also the question – can you live with this person for the two, three, four years – in the case of Norman Sherry, when he wrote about Graham Greene, for the 30 years – it will take to research and write the book? If your publisher suggests someone that doesn't appeal to you, don't even think of doing it, however big the advance. I was asked to do Dorothy Sayers and Mother Teresa – but for some reason I could never put my finger on, I didn't want to spend all that time with either of them, admirable and interesting though they both are. There was not the strange, necessarily one-sided personal rapport that is essential if the book is to be more than a summary of fact and received opinion.

So how do you choose? Again I make the analogy with marriage. You choose someone who excites you, with whom you have fallen at least slightly in love. Then you hope that the fates are kind and that if they are alive they will let you do it, if they are dead that their estate, or whoever is in charge of their papers, gives you permission: that you then get co-operation and that when you're ready you will get interest from a publisher. Personally I have no wish to do a biography publicised as 'the official biography' as there is then always the possibility that pressure will be brought to bear on the writer to take a particular line – and that biographers should do their best to be unprejudiced is, of course, crucial.

So for me it goes without saying that a biographer must at the very least like their subject. I know there have been biographies written about people who dislike their subject, but I think it must be exceedingly painful for the writer – imagine choosing to spend all that time with someone you dislike – and intolerable for the friends and relatives of the subjects. I have never seen why Graham Lord wrote his biography of John Mortimer. It must indeed have been painful for the biographer that the subject withdrew his permission after he had started work, but surely he cannot have got much pleasure from allowing such a stream of vitriol to escape?

There is no doubt about it, the relationship between biographer and subject is very strange. It is the ultimate in one-sided relationships. A biographer may come to know more about their subject than anyone else living, yet the subject knows little or nothing about you. Of course things will change as the months roll into years, but the balance of the relationship does not change. The biographer seeks always to know and understand more about their subject – any passing reference, any new fact – while the writer herself can, if she so wishes, retain her privacy. This is a blessing to the shy violets, a welcome cover behind which they are relieved to hide. Perhaps that is one of the reasons people write biographies.

Further, a biographer spends so much time with their subject. One's entire working life for the time it takes to complete the book is devoted to this one person – their lives, their thoughts, the subjects in which they were interested, their friends, their relations and descendants. Sometimes they do not wish to be forgotten at night and may appear in your dreams.

People often ask what the difference is in writing between someone living and someone dead. I have written about two people I knew and met, two older contemporaries I never met, one person who died over four hundred years ago. The main difference is, obviously, that you cannot talk directly to the dead, but otherwise I find there is less difference than you might expect.

Is writing biography a form of cowardice? I have always been aware that I am in a way hiding behind my subjects. I can indulge my interest while hiding under the umbrella of my subject's deep knowledge and experience. I have not the skill, the nerve or the confidence to tackle these great matters – illness, death, apartheid, mysticism – myself, so I take refuge in another's wisdom. And how many biographers write autobiographies? I suspect that writing about other people is in fact writing about oneself indirectly. You cannot but be there, but you do not have to reveal yourself totally. You hide under their greatness. What happens when a writer happy to explore the lives of their subjects turns to revealing something of their own lives, as in this book, is, of course, another matter.

This leads to the question of what publishers sometimes call the 'authorial voice.' How much do biographers allow themselves to be seen? In a way the highest compliment is to be told that you have let the subject tell their own story, that you have kept yourself out of the way. But you know it isn't true. Every judgement you make, every judgement you dare not make, is in fact a reflection on the author. Even the way you select the areas you cover gives away something about you. For instance I write mainly about people with some sort of concern for spirituality and religion, but I am not an academic theologian. That shows in my approach. My own passion is for experience and for story. What a reviewer called 'the white-knuckled spiritual ride.' I love to try to express the drama in another life, to try to let the reader share the experience. However, when confidence fails and you are uncertain of making some judgement, you can quote the words of others: every biographer does this, but do it too much and you can incur the charge that the authorial voice is too weak.

Do you tell everything, 'warts and all'? Of course you do – what sort of a biography would it be that didn't? Hagiography – and no one wants that today. Besides, in practice there is not a problem. If you are as close to your subject as I am suggesting you become, if you are devoted to him or her, admiring and loving, why should you deny them a few faults? There is rarely a problem with simply telling the truth. Cicely Saunders was amazing in this way. I was not entirely flattering about her, but when she read the draft she corrected every point of fact – she even pointed out that a dress she was wearing was three-quarter length not full length as I had written – but she did not ask me to change one single point of judgement. Tutu was the same, though he did not take such a detailed interest in the book. I think the same would be true of Teresa, Bede and Abhishiktananda. On the other hand I heard the other day of someone wanting their biography written but unable to find a biographer because everyone knew she would want a finger in the pie along every page.

I was talking to someone recently who put it beautifully. She asked me if I idealised my subjects and I said of course not, do you idealise your husband? And she said no, of course not, I love him far too much. So we end where we began. Biography is of course based on facts, but it is also about story and about relationship.

11

'God is One, but His Names are Many'

These five people with whom I spent so long – extraordinary Christians like Cicely Saunders, Teresa of Avila, Desmond Tutu, Bede Griffiths and Abhishiktananda – all believed in God: but what God? What did they mean by God? Part of the excitement of living so close to these people was to be given the chance to look as deeply as one was able into their understanding of God, to learn about the quality of that relationship and what aspects they loved, worshipped, tried to emulate; the aspects from which they drew most comfort. I did not at the time think that, in choosing these five subjects, I was following any particular trail, but looking back on those years spent in their company I realise that I was influenced by them, shaped by them, more than I recognised at the time; that I cannot trace my own changing relationship to God in the ever-changing, increasingly secular, twentieth and twenty-first centuries without recognising the part played by these five people.

Cicely Saunders is known by her works, for St Christopher's, the Hospice for the Dying she started in 1967, is the incarnation of a religious and medical ideal. Her Christian life began at the evangelical church of All Souls, Langham Place, but her vision of God broadened until in her sixties she embraced all faiths in the conviction that they led to the same God. In fact she was probably the first to use the phrase 'of all faiths or of none' when describing people who were welcome at the Hospice.

Soon after the official opening of the Hospice the staff held their first Communion Service, two dying patients being wheeled down from their wards in their beds. Thus was their faith immediately and publicly expressed. Cicely expressed her belief in the oneness of God with disarming simplicity: 'We are not emphasising that there is just one way but rather that there is one person coming in many ways.'[1]   And she was drawn to those who, like her old friend and patient Louie, when asked what was the first thing she would say to God, replied that she would say, 'I know you.'   Cicely's Christianity was also essentially practical, believing that, 'If God calls, he also enables', and responding to God's call in a very down-to-earth way. By responding to this call she revolutionised the way in which society cares for the ill, the dying and the bereaved and left society forever in her debt.

Desmond Tutu endearingly admits that though he was always a deeply committed Christian, he didn't have very high or noble reasons for going to theological college. This, however, is what he did – he later referred to 'God grabbing me by the scruff of my neck.'[2] It could not have been an easy decision, because Tutu was an exceptionally able student and in those days of apartheid black priests occupied a lowly place in white eyes. They were shepherded and controlled by white priests, able only to eat the crumbs from their table. There is even a story of a black canon being forbidden to drink tea in a white man's sitting room.

Though Tutu is most known and respected for his courageous stand against apartheid, he is also an extraordinarily loving man in very ordinary ways. His spirituality is incarnational: 'You can't love people and not visit them,' he says, 'you can't love them unless you know them and you can't know them unless you visit them. A good shepherd knows his sheep by name.'[3]   When I was researching his life in General Theological

---

[1]   Shirley du Boulay, *Cicely Saunders: Founder of the Modern Hospice Movement*, p.161.
[2]   Shirley du Boulay, *Voice of the Voiceless* (Hodder and Stoughton, 1988), p.45.
3   Ibid. p.56.

Seminary in New York I was impressed by the most trivial of memories about him. It was shared with me by a young man who had a very bad cold on the first occasion that he had met Tutu. A year later they met again and immediately Tutu asked if he recovered all right from his nasty cold. On a more personal note, when my husband died Tutu sent me a kind note and an enormous bunch of flowers.

With St Teresa of Avila I went back 400 years, moved from the Anglican Church to the Roman Catholic and from South Africa to Spain. Teresa's idea of God was a very literal understanding of a powerful God – she was, for instance, convinced that it was God who sent her a serious illness in order that she should have leisure to consider what she should do with her life. It was through this illness that she talked to an uncle who provided the turning point in her indecision and, admitting her motivation was 'servile fear rather than love', she decided to force herself to become a nun. And later, when another turning point came, it was in direct conversation with her God. 'I threw myself down beside Him, shedding floods of tears and begging him to give me strength once and for all so that I might not offend Him … I believe I told Him then that I would not rise from that spot until He granted me what I was beseeching of Him.'[4] This moment became known as her 'fiat' – the moment when she gave herself totally to Christ.

Teresa is still much loved and admired; she was so intensely human, so extraordinarily ordinary. Her passionate faith in God allowed her to move naturally between two worlds that for many people are contradictory: the outer world of negotiation, tension and stress as she founded convents all over Spain and the inner world of the progress of the soul to God.

---

[4] Shirley du Boulay, *Teresa of Avila: An Extraordinary Life*, (Hodder and Stoughton, 1991), p. 42.

Her love of God is expressed most famously in a short poem known as Teresa's Bookmark:

> Let nothing disturb you
> Let nothing frighten you
> All things pass away
> God never changes.
> Patience obtains all things.
> He who has God
> Finds he lacks nothing;
> God alone suffices.

Perhaps today that, above all, is what we can learn from her – to find God in everything and everywhere. Not to categorise and divide. The other day I heard a priest say from the pulpit, 'We stand together in the presence of God ...' I had the feeling that he meant there was some external reason for God's presence, like the fact that we were in a church, and I wanted to ask him when we were *not* in the presence of God. Teresa would never have said such a thing.

I was touched, deeply touched and profoundly influenced, by these three people, by their thoughts on the nature of God and by the way they gave their lives to incarnating those values for the benefit of others, to improve the world in which they lived. To some extent I related to them personally and identified with their problems and their longings, and there was no doubting the depth of affection I developed for them, but it was not until 1994, when I started researching the life of the Benedictine monk Bede Griffiths, that I felt a real sense of identification; that I knew that here was someone who was saying what I had been, if only half-consciously, thinking; trying to explore further the very realms where I longed to go, where I had been given a brief, though timeless and unforgettable, glimpse.

It started with the similarity I saw between Bede's school-boy experience and my own, at roughly the same age.[5] For Bede it was the sense of awe, so great that he 'hardly dared to look on the face of the sky, because it seemed as though it was but a veil before the face of God.' Bede Griffiths spent his life seeking to re-live his early experience and I too long to experience my glimpse of 'oneness' again. But these experiences do not come at a call, they do not respond to even the most ardent pleadings. Yet we live in hope. It might be today. It might be tomorrow. It might – of course - be never. Yet once one has had an experience like that it is never forgotten – it is woven into the tapestry of one's personality and one's life and can never be unpicked from the rest of the picture – nor would one want it to be.

But there was more that led me to identify with Bede Griffiths – as indeed have countless people in recent years. He was among the first in the twentieth century to recognise God as Mother, he favoured married clergy, he was a pioneer in trying to bring about the union of East and West, and was a man who was deeply aware of the tension between the opposites. This tension found reconciliation in the hours he spent in meditation and in his conviction that all opposites are reconciled in truth, since they are all partial expressions of one reality. That, for instance, the Hindu experience of God should be related to the Christian doctrine of creation, the Trinity and the incarnation. This was crucial in his attitude to the ashram he founded:

> A Christian ashram, if it is to be worthy of the name, must be a place where a meeting can take place in 'the cave of the heart' between the Christian experience of God through faith in Jesus Christ and the Hindu experience of

---

[5] See pp 2 and 6

'Brahman' the One 'without a second,' the Ground of all creation and the 'Atman,' the Spirit, dwelling in the heart of every man.

It is in God that all opposites meet.

Bede Griffiths was a man of his time. In fact after his death one leading article referred to him as 'a lonely trail-blazer'[6] and the *National Catholic Reporter* wrote: 'Even at age 86 and on the edge of death Benedictine Fr Bede Griffiths was still running so far ahead of the pack that his life's momentum will quicken him for many springs to come.'[7]

After writing Bede's biography, I considered writing about Swami Abhishiktananda, the French Benedictine who was one of the founders of Shantivanam, the ashram Bede made famous and where he spent the last 25 years of his life. However when Abhishiktananda's great friend, the Anglican priest Murray Rogers, pressed me to do so and the wistful ponderings became real opportunity, I was terrified, especially as a theologian friend had said, 'Any biography of Abhishiktananda would have to be a theological biography.' I am no theologian, so that scared the wits out of me. But the hardest thing – and the reason I was right to be frightened of doing it – was not so much theology as to try to do justice to someone who had experienced such extraordinary spiritual heights and depths. It was Murray who eventually persuaded me to do it and I am endlessly grateful to him for leading me towards four years of such richness as I tried to swim in the same waters as this great man.

I never met Abhishiktananda, but by writing his biography he has become a friend and spiritual mentor as surely as if I had met him. I think we, living in a time when spirituality is so diffused and so complex, are extraordinarily lucky to have

---

[6] *America*, 5-12 June 1993.
[7] Tim McCarthy, *National Catholic Reporter,* 21 May 1993.

such a figure speaking for our time. While Bede was a great communicator, bringing East and West together with the ease and confidence of one at home in both worlds, Abhishiktananda takes us even deeper, even further, into the spiritual world that is, ultimately, common to all faiths, all cultures.

In fact I found that by following Abhishiktananda's life, with its continual emphasis on experience, I did not need to worry too much about theology, for his life was its expression. He was following his instinct for God with tenacity and an almost reckless bravery; he was courageous in his spiritual exploration, honest in his account of it. Following the twists and turns in search of the Holy Grail is as enthralling a journey as a human being can make, and like any journey with such a prize, it is dangerous. I knew that in writing about him I would have to enter into the tensions that tore him apart, particularly of being a European who fell in love with India and, much more fiercely and causing him far more pain, being a devout Christian equally drawn to Hinduism. I have not yet assimilated all that I learnt from him and I don't think that I ever will. He knew both the deepest spiritual agony and climbed the highest peaks. He experienced so deeply his oneness with God that he wrote in his diary, 'As long as I feel two, it is exile.'[8]

One can hardly talk about a desire for oneness with God or the oneness of God, the Being without a second, without wondering what we make of the fact that God has so many names? Is it an attempt to claim an aspect of the universal as one's own? We want to pin him down, to personalise him (or her I need hardly say). Is it like the need for baptism in human beings? As with

---

[8]   Abhishiktananda, *Spiritual Diary* (ISPCK, 1998), p.32.

human beings – one of the first questions we ask of a new baby is what will he/she be called?

We laugh at the parents who gave their unfortunate baby eleven names – the entire local football team – but many religions go further than that. Hinduism claimed in the Rig Veda, written about a thousand years before Christ: 'They have called him Indra, Mitra, Varuna, Agni, and the divine fine-winged Garuda. They speak of Indra, Yama, Matrarisvan: the One Being sages call by many names.'[9] And of course the Qur'an famously lists 99 Names of God. I am beginning to think that the more names there are for God, the more it speaks of the one God, who defies limitation – just as an excess of love for the loved one sometimes leads to a thousand pet names. God may be worshipped in many different forms, but why should we fight over it? The defense of a particular idea of God leads to dispute, division, even death, but there CAN only be one God at the top of the mountain.

We catch glimpses of this one God, this mysterious 'being', in relationships, in art, in nature, in prayer. Sometimes out of a clear sky, walking past a postbox in a busy street. When struggling to tie a shoelace. God, as Abhishiktananda wrote to a friend, is just as present 'in the preparation of a tasty soup or the careful handling of a railway-train as he is in our most beautiful meditations.'[10] And to another he wrote: 'God is beyond all notions. They are only spring-boards to be used for diving – and the spring board is not the lake.'[11]

---

[9] *Rig Veda 1.164.46*

[10] James Stewart, *Swami Abhishiktananda: His life told through his letters* (ISPCK, 1989), foreword by Donald Nicholl, p.x.

[11] Letter from Abhishiktananda to Odette Baumer, 7 July1968.

So I had the great good fortune to spend all those years in the company of people passionately drawn to some of the many aspects of God; most of all drawn to the oneness of God. And that has always been central for me, even before I was aware of it, long before I had any language for it. I have always found the idea of God incarnated in Jesus Christ hard, almost impossible, to grasp; I was even further from understanding the avenging God of the Old Testament. Yet for many years I read the Bible daily, and sometimes I came across lines that moved me at a depth beyond expression. For instance, from Psalm 139, 'the darkness and the light are both alike to thee.'[12] For months – years – after discovering this line it resounded within me. In fact it still does. Here was the God of the Opposites in heroic mould, rising even above the daily and natural cycle of night and day. If it is possible to see such powerful, elemental opposites as one, then perhaps it is theoretically possible to see the oneness beyond the apparent distinctions between men and women, living and dying, rich and poor, full and empty.

And who or what *is* that oneness? Is it the one spoken of in that miraculous passage from Proverbs:

> The Lord possessed me in the beginning of his way, before his works of old. I was set up from everlasting, from the beginning, or ever the earth was. When there were no depths, I was brought forth; when there were no fountains abounding with water. Before the mountains were settled, before the hills was I brought forth.[13]

Who is the 'I' who was possessed by the Lord? Is it me? Is it you? It is all sentient beings? Is it life itself?

---

[12] Psalm 139:12. I am using the Authorized Version of the Bible as it was the first version I read and, for me, is by far the most beautiful and the most rich in meaning.

[13] Proverbs 8:22-25.

In the New Testament I read and re-read the lines from St John's Gospel: 'That they all may be one; as thou, Father, art in me, and I in thee, that they also may be one in us.'[14] These lines speak so directly; one does not even need to understand exactly what they mean.

So various ideas – the God beyond the opposites, God as the 'I' who had always been with the Lord from before the beginning of time, the oneness of the mystics – swam around my confused head. I was in absolutely no doubt that the word God had some meaning, that I believed in something, but for decades I had no idea what it was. Then suddenly, not so long ago, it struck me – what about the idea that God is Being? Just that.

When this first dawned on me, that God and Being were the same, that God *was* Being … well it knocked me over, it delighted me, I wondered why I had never heard anyone say it before and I kept the thought to myself. On the one hand it was so obvious that what was there to be said about it? On the other no one else seemed to be saying it, I had never come across the idea in the writings of others, so had I just failed to understand something? Had I just missed it? Or had I got it seriously wrong? I started exploring the history of the idea. I was in little doubt that the poets and mystics would have no problems with it, but I needed to find out what theologians had said.

I will never forget that wonderful moment when I found theological backing for the idea of God as Being. It was about five years ago. I was reading Thomas Merton's autobiography, *The Seven Storey Mountain*, and I came across this amazing passage. Merton tells how in February 1937, before he entered the monastery of Gethsemani, he was wandering aimlessly round a bookshop, when he impulsively picked up a copy of a book. It was *The Spirit of Medieval Philosophy* by Etienne Gilson. The great realisation he got from these pages was one of the

---

[14] John 17:21.

peak moments of his years as a layman. It is contained in one word, the word *aseitas,* which he describes as 'one of those dry, outlandish compounds that the scholastic philosophers were so prone to use.' It comes from the medieval word *aseity*, meaning 'underived' or 'of an independent existence.' And of whom or what can that be said? This is what Merton writes about it:

> In this one word, which can be applied to God alone, and which expresses His most characteristic attribute, I discovered an entirely new concept of God – a concept which showed me at once that the belief of Catholics was by no means the vague and rather superstitious hangover from an unscientific age that I believed it to be. On the contrary, here was a notion of God that was at the same time deep, precise, simple, and accurate and, what is more, charged with implications which I could not even begin to appreciate, but which I could at least dimly estimate, even with my own lack of philosophical training.[15]

He goes on to look at the meaning of the word.

> *'Aseitas'* is the English equivalent in a transliteration: aseity – simply means the power of a being to exist absolutely in virtue of itself, not as caused by itself, but as requiring no cause, no other justification for its existence except that its very nature is to exist. There can be only one such Being: that is God. And to say that God exists *a se*, of and by reason of Himself, is merely to say that God is Being Itself. *Ego sum qui sum.* And this means that God must enjoy 'complete independence not only as regards everything outside but also as regards everything within Himself.[16]

---

15 Thomas Merton, *The Seven Storey Mountain* (Harcourt, Inc., 1948), p.189.
16 Ibid.

Chambers Dictionary defines aseity as 'self-origination' from the Latin 'a' (from) and 'se' (oneself). The Shorter Oxford Dictionary's entry is 'Underived or independent existence'. Merton made a pencil note at the top of the page: 'Aseity of God – God is being *per se*.'

This realisation had a profound effect on Merton; indeed he said it was to revolutionize his entire life. He realised that he had never really known what Christians meant by God, simply taking it for granted that God was 'a noisy and dramatic and passionate character, a vague, jealous hidden being, the objectification of all their own strivings and subjective ideals.' He was also impossible, for, in the theology Merton had taken in with his mother's milk, God was 'infinite and yet finite, perfect and imperfect, eternal and yet changing'. Now he knew. He knew that God was Being itself and that we must not, and need not, look outside God for a cause for the existence of God.

Once Merton had given this word, so new to me, both theological and etymological meaning, I found the idea in other places. For instance I wondered if Merton had read Heidegger, who in the early twentieth century pointed out that western philosophy, since Plato, has tended to approach this question of being in terms of *a* being, rather than asking about Being itself. They looked at the noun rather than the verb.

Then there was the phrase 'the Ground of our Being', much used in the early sixties, late in the life of Paul Tillich, the famous systematic theologian who coined the phrase and worked on its implications. At the time the phrase resounded in my ears and excited me in a vague sort of way, but I did not really know what it was about.

Now I began to see what he meant. If I may attempt to paraphrase the great Tillich, he sees the concept of Being in three ways. First in the doctrine of God, where God is called 'the being as being' or 'the ground and the power of being'. In human beings, where the distinction is made between their essential and existential being. And in the doctrine of Christ, where he is called the manifestation of the New Being, the actualisation of which is the work of the divine Spirit.[17] In Tillich's own words:

> It is the expression of the experience of being over against non-being. Therefore, it can be described as the power of being which resists non-being. For this reason, the medieval philosophers called being the basic *transcendentale*, beyond the universal and the particular...
>
> The same word, the emptiest of all concepts when taken as an abstraction, becomes the most meaningful of all concepts when it is understood as the power of being in everything that has being.[18]

At about the same time Teilhard de Chardin was writing his *Hymn of the Universe*, first published in French in 1961:

> Lord...You came down into me by means of a tiny scrap of created reality; and then, suddenly, you unfurled your immensity before my eyes and displayed yourself to me as Universal Being.
>
> So the basic mystical intuition issues in the discovery of a supra-real unity diffused through the immensity of the world.[19]

I began to see this idea in other places. When I was writing about the French Benedictine Abhishiktananda, I was excited beyond telling by this passage, from a letter written in 1953.

---

[17] *Systematic Theology,* 3 volumes (University of Chicago Press, 1951 – 63), Vol. 2, p. 10.

[18] *Systematic Theology Vol. 2*, p.11.

[19] *Hymn of the Universe*, Pierre Teilhard de Chardin, trs. Simon Bartholomew (Collins, 1965), p.18.

Being is inexpressible. In the within there is only Being. And the distinctions whether in God in the full possession of Being, or amongst the creatures in the participation of Being, have nothing to do with Being. There is no BEING and BEING.[20]

(What is not apparent in the spoken word is the way, in that crucial last line, he writes the first 'ETRE' in big capitals, then 'ETRE' slightly smaller.) The next year Abhishiktananda wrote in his Diary: 'God is only another name of being, of being when it is looked in the face … But can God look himself in the face? God does not look at himself; if he could look at himself, how would he still be God?'[21]

The realization that God is Being contributed to the extraordinary nature of Abhishiktananda's last days on earth. He had a bad heart attack, walking in the street by himself. For some time he lay on the pavement, until help came. He wrote to his friend Murray Rogers of this:

Really a door opened in heaven when I was lying on the pavement. But a heaven which was not the opposite of earth, something which was neither life nor death, but simply 'being', 'awakening' … beyond all myths and symbols.[22]

It blows the mind, doesn't it? The great spiritual moment of awakening, enlightenment, whatever one prefers to call it, was,

---

[20] Henri Le Saux, *Lettres d'un sannyasi chretien a Joseph Lemarie*, tr. Vicky Clouston (Les Editions du Cerf, 1999), p.78.
[21] Abhishiktananda, *Ascent to the Depth of the Heart*, tr. David Fleming and James Stuart (ISPCK, 1988), p.95.
[22] Letter to Murray Rogers, 4 October 1973, taken from James Stuart, *Swami Abhishiktananda: His Life told through his letters* (ISPCK, 1989), p. 349.

for this Frenchman, also a time when he experienced simply 'being'. Pure, in a way simple, 'being.'

❧

Once captivated by this idea, assured that it was not just my own crazy notion, I saw it everywhere. There can only be one God – and that is Being. So I found the same idea in many places. In the Upanishads:

> He moves, and he moves not. He is far, and he is near. He is within all, and he is outside all.
>
> Who sees all beings in his own Self, and his own Self in all beings, loses all fear.
>
> When a sage sees this great Unity and his Self has become all beings, what delusion and what sorrow can ever be near him?[23]

I found it too in the Chinese character *wu*, signifying both 'absolute being' and 'awakening, enlightenment'. So to be enlightened is to experience pure being. I found it in the Bible, especially in the famous I AM's. When God commissioned Moses to return to Egypt and free the Israelites, Moses asked:

> What is his name? What shall I say unto them? And God said unto Moses, I AM THAT I AM; and he said, Thus shalt thou say unto the children of Israel, 'I AM hath sent me unto you.' [24]

I found it in the God of Etty Hillesum, who died in Auschwitz. She wrote in her diary, 'And that part of myself, that deepest and richest part in which I repose, is what I call "God".' In

---

[23] *The Upanishads*, trs. Juan Mascaro (Penguin Classics, 1965), p.49.

[24] Exodus 3:13-14, Authorised Bible.

Alan Watts: 'There is only this *now*. It does not come from anywhere; it is not going anywhere. It is not permanent, but it is not impermanent. Though moving it is always still. When we try to touch it, it seems to run away.' In fact you find it in all writing on the importance of living in the present. 'There is *no* becoming. There is just *being*.' This was written a few years ago by Brian Pierce, an American Dominican.

There may be many ways up the mountain, but we cannot travel them all at once. Eventually we have to choose. But whichever way we choose, surely the view from the top is the same? Surely the God is the same?

The word God is overused and misunderstood. For years I have been uncomfortable with it, unable to find another. Yet while there are so many names for God, nobody has yet come up with another that fills all our needs. In the end there are no names, as the fourth-century Cappadocian, Father Gregory Nazianzen, well knew.

> By what name can I call upon you,
> You who are beyond all names?
> You are both all things and none; not a part yet not the whole.
> All names are given to you and yet none can comprehend you,
> How shall I name you then, O You, the Beyond-all-name?

12

After the Millennium

On 31 December 1999, groups of people all over the world gathered to celebrate the Millennium. Most of us were affected by millennium fever, compelled to celebrate in some way, meet our friends, throw a party – but what were we celebrating? A date. A date that is believed to honour the birth of Jesus Christ 2000 years earlier, though in all probability not the right date. It was indeed an excuse for a party, but it's hard to see any way in which it reflected the teachings of the founder of Christianity. But while it was not easy to find spiritual significance in the fun and partying, the millennium celebrations did do one thing very thoroughly – they said a firm goodbye to the twentieth century and ushered in the twenty-first.

All right, so it's still only a date, but dates are useful things. They help to give shape to history, put brackets round movements in art, political regimes, writing, scientific discovery. We only have to hear someone compare fashion in the eighteenth century with today's fashions, than we think of opulence, wigs, embroidery, bustles, straight-backed chairs and formal introductions.

So, just a few years into the twenty-first century, are there any definable trends in spirituality? What are we taking on from the twentieth century and what are we discarding? Where – dare we even ask the question – are we heading?

As we entered the new century I was already in my sixties and had quite a clear idea of the kind of spirituality that spoke to me. So in a sense I was no longer actively searching, perhaps no longer a 'child of my time', but I remained aware of what was going on around me spiritually – that awareness had been part of my life for too long for it to be swiftly relegated. So I heard about conferences, such as that organised by the Wrekin Trust and called 'The Emerging Spiritual Revolution', but though I was interested and tempted to go, in the event I did not. I knew that Eckhart Tolle, a man I deeply admire and whose books are amongst my most treasured, was speaking in London, but somehow I was content to read his words and did not get myself organised to go and hear him speak. I was still occasionally tempted along the by-ways – for a while I was involved with an American self-healing system called 'The Healing Codes' in an attempt to heal my deafness, a condition that has been creeping up on me since John's death, but the curious juxtaposition of hand gestures and thoughts did nothing for me. I met the extraordinary Douglas Harding, who expressed the feeling of 'no self' that mystics aspire to in a classic work first published in 1961 called *On Having No Head*. I was honoured to meet him, but did not take my interest any further.

Even though I used to talk in public myself, I have always preferred the written to the spoken word and have few regrets about the talks and conferences that I have not attended. But there are two people, active in both the twentieth and the twenty-first centuries, whom I feel sad to have missed. One is Mother Meera,[1] who had such a powerful effect on the friend to whom this book is dedicated, and is believed by her followers to be an embodiment of the Divine Mother. She was born in India in 1960 and for many years has received thousands of visitors in darshan, when she simply touches each person's head and looks deep into their eyes. She says of her work, 'Like electricity, the Light is everywhere, but one must know how to activate

---

[1] See p. 44.

it. I have come for that.'[2] I know several people who have received her touch and there is no doubt that they experienced a powerful and extraordinary force.

Another Indian spiritual leader, Mata Amritanandamayi Devi, is known simply as Amma, 'Mother', and is often described as 'the Hugging Mama'. From a young age she would take poor people food and clothing from her own home and, now in her sixties, she is widely respected for her humanitarian work. Like Mother Meera, she is, however, known most for the power of her presence and of her touch. Since 1987 she has been travelling the world meeting people and responding to their sorrow by embracing them – it is believed that over the last 30 years she has embraced more than 32 million people. 'If you can touch people you can touch the world', she says, with beautiful simplicity.

She does not see her embracing of strangers as in any way strange, nor does she distinguish between hugging a man or a woman, saying, 'I don't see anyone different from my own self.' Her love in action reflects the greatest mystical teaching. In her own words:

> There is one truth that shines through all of creation. Rivers and mountains, plants and animals, the sun, the moon and the stars, you and I – all are expressions of this one Reality.[3]

What a change from what was once Roman Catholicism, the remote priest speaking in Latin with his back to the people. Now it is physical touch, warmth, the recognition of eye contact, that draws people in their millions, moves them and leaves them feeling strengthened and supported. I am slightly surprised at myself for not making the effort to meet these

---

[2] *Answers, Part I*, Mother Meera, ISBN 0-9622973-3-X.
[3] http://en.wikipedia.org/wiki/Mata_Amritanandamayi

remarkable women; for not attempting to experience firsthand this manifestation of the spirituality of our time. Is it laziness that prevents me? I would not deny that charge, but beyond everything it is meditation that draws me.

❦

As the new century dawned I was still going to Mass regularly, still trying to regard myself as a Christian, but my instinct is less for liturgy and ritual than for silence and meditation; my nourishment lies there. This is true for an ever-increasing number of people. There are regular meditation groups meeting in village halls, churches, private houses anywhere 'where two or three may be gathered together.' There are ways of meditating in the Christian tradition – the Julian Groups, the World Community for Christian Meditation, the Ignatian exercises; there are Buddhist practices such as Vipassana, also known as 'Insight' meditation; mantra meditations such as the Maharishi's Transcendental Meditation. But the most popular and the fastest growing meditation practice in this century is Mindfulness, popularised in the West by Jon Kabat-Zinn, who founded the Mindfulness-Based Stress Reduction programme at the University of Massachusetts in 1979.

Mindfulness meditation has an astonishing similarity to the Maharishi's meditation, which drew me so powerfully back in 1960 – and was in fact my introduction to meditation. As Transcendental Meditation has its roots in Hinduism, so Mindfulness is based on one of the eight teachings of the Noble Eightfold Path of Buddhism; both focus on attention and awareness, both are often taught independently of religion, both involve trying to live in the present moment, both encourage research into the effects of meditation and both are found to have therapeutic applications, reducing anxiety, depression and stress. And, in a sense, most critically, both appeal to a twenty-first century mentality, which seeks a spiritual dimension but is disillusioned by institutional religion.

If I were looking for a meditation practice it is to mindfulness I would turn, but spirituality for me still means to go East and I have found there a practice which sustains and delights me. For a while I studied Sanskrit, in an attempt to better understand the great Hindu classics like the Upanishads; I went to retreats organised by the Bede Griffiths Sangha, charmingly called 'Hermits', but my loyalty remains with Zen, that great treasure of the Far East, which I still value more than anything else I have yet encountered. Much of the practice is, of course, done in the quiet of one's own home, but I love to go to the weekly meetings and on the three and five day retreats, with long hours of meditation in the company of others. I did not tackle the three month retreat that many of my braver friends undertook one summer, for even the shorter retreats tax my back to its limits of pain with the long hours of silent sitting. But it is worth it.

❦

I am aware of a confusion in my tenses as I write of the present century. While the turn of the century is now 14 years ago and it has seemed natural to refer to it in the past tense, there comes a point when the past becomes the present. So in considering what is going on around me now, in the spiritual revolution that the twenty-first century is most surely witnessing, I must use the present tense. What place do spirituality and religion have now, in the lives of those around me?   Where is Christianity in these turbulent, uncertain times?   And where do I find myself in the endless choices that surround me?

The most apparent aspect of twenty-first-century Christianity, and the one easiest to record, is of course the decline in church attendance. The numerous surveys conducted on this subject seem to fall into broad agreement. Russia, Scandinavia and Japan are among the countries where less that 10 per cent of the population go regularly to church, while some 80 per cent of people in Nigeria and Ireland are regular attenders. At 44 per cent the United States falls somewhere in the middle, and Great Britain comes lower at about a quarter of the population. These numbers are set to sink further as the process of secularisation continues: in fact the United Kingdom is now described as multi-faith, secularised, or sometimes a post-Christian society.

Certainly that is how I experience the twenty-first century in the UK. Even though I know a great many people for whom their Christian faith is deeply important, it does not seem possible to claim that this is a predominantly Christian country any longer. I am not sure I even want to do so, for in a country whose foreign-born population increased by over 50 per cent in the first decade of the new millennium,[4] we surely want to honour the faiths of all, rather than for one religion to claim numerical superiority. Prince Charles understood that when, eight years into the new century, he repeated a declaration he had already floated once to a public, who at the time were slightly mystified, that when he becomes King he would like to take the title Defender of Faith, rather than Defender of *the* Faith, to reflect Britain's multi-cultural society. I think we understand him rather better now, though whether he can overcome such obstacles as the amendment of the 1953 Royal Titles Act is another matter.

I do wish, though, that the same respect was given to Christianity as to those of other faiths; the image of the Christian priest being offered sugar for his tea – 'one lump or two, Vicar?' – dies hard. It is often noticeable how the greatest respect is shown for anyone claiming to be a Muslim, but very little for

---

[4] Michael Rendall, John Salt, *Focus on People and Migration* (Palgrave Macmillan, 2005), pp.131–152.

people describing themselves as Christian. Pages of newsprint are devoted to the annual fasting of Muslims at Ramadan and to the celebrations of its ending at Eid, while the birth and death and resurrection of Christ are recorded more by the pleasures of secular national holidays and a great deal of eating and drinking than by any interest in their real significance.

We are so concerned with political correctness, so fearful of offending non-Christian susceptibilities, that we conceal Christian practice and symbolism in cloaks of shame. In 2006 it was noted that three out of four employers no longer put up Christmas decorations in the workplace for fear of offending political sensitivities. Christian images are fast disappearing from greeting cards in an attempt to please non-Christians; the Royal Mail has been slowly removing any Christian references from Christmas stamps – now there are so few that when they are found there is rejoicing and Christians urge each other to buy them. Christian nativity plays in schools are being replaced by secular tales to avoid upsetting pupils of other faiths; there are attempts to make wearing crosses at work illegal.

There are of course endless arguments over the wish of some Muslim women to wear the niqab. But at least this issue is the subject of a healthy discussion, and most people would agree with the views of a forthright journalist like Joan Smith:

> The demand by a small number of Muslim women to cover their faces in all circumstances clearly impacts on the rights of others, and requires a robust response. If a woman wants to wear the niqab in Tesco or on the 94 bus, I think we should let her get on with it. But when she wants to work with members of the public or becomes involved in the criminal justice system, that's a completely different matter.[5]

---

[5] Joan Smith, *Independent*, 10 October 2013.

The cowering attempts made by some Christians to please, even at the cost of symbols of their faith, is a cause for shame and it led, in 2007, to a debate in Parliament on the spread in Britain of 'Christianophobia' – the hatred of Christianity. There was a 90-minute debate, but no vote. What indeed could the proposal have been?

The irony is that many non-Christians would positively prefer Christians to live their religious lives with pride rather than with shame. Even the most devout and respected Christians can be tainted by this fear. There is a story that the Benedictine monk Bede Griffiths, when he was living in India, felt he ought to celebrate the Christian Eucharist with a low profile, until the local Hindus and Muslims, amazed and rather shocked, said, 'But we *want* you to proclaim your faith, just as we proclaim ours.' I long for Christianity to be respected even while my own faithfulness to it weakens every year. I long for Christians to be proud. Whether we are Christians or not, Christianity is the background to two thousand years of western civilization.

❦

Yet there are areas where Christianity flourishes. If you are depressed by the sight of empty pews, go to Somerset. Go to the charismatic conference, where the New Wine Conference is held in a huge tent at the Royal Bath and Wells Showground. In August 2013 a week-long conference was attended by between ten and fifteen thousand enthusiastic evangelical Christians, praising God in the pouring rain.

And two Christian leaders are doing much for the image of Christianity, indeed for the image of religion itself. Justin Welby, the main speaker at the New Wine Conference, was enthroned as Archbishop of Canterbury in 2013 and has already made an impression. He is not only a devout evangelical Christian, but having worked for 11 years in the oil industry has a knowledge of business that is unusual in a church leader.

It seems unbelievable that the Church is taking on big business, but it is true. Not long after he became Archbishop he stood up to the payday loan company Wonga, who charge extortionate interest rates. But this Archbishop did not just moralise, he told the chief executive of Wonga: 'We're not in the business of trying to legislate you out of existence; we're trying to compete you out of existence.' He then supported these fighting words by suggesting that the Church of England could offer its facilities and the expertise of its congregations to offer financial services and bring down the cost of borrowing.

The Catholic Church also has a new leader who is inspiring respect in secular as well as religious areas – indeed Pope Francis was quickly dubbed the 'Pope of Surprises'. This is a man who underwent an extraordinary conversion from authoritarian conservative to friend of the poor, and one of the surprises is that the shadows in his past somehow increase his credibility. Here is a Pope who does not attempt to hide his limitations; indeed the early days of his papacy were filled with examples of his humility. He refused the first-class ticket the Vatican had sent him and travelled from Buenos Aires to Rome in economy class; straight after his election he spurned the official chauffeur-driven limousine and took the bus; when it came to choosing papal vestments he chose, not the velvet cape trimmed with ermine and the red shoes beloved by his predecessor, Benedict XVI, but pointed at his shabby old black shoes saying that these would be fine for him. Most significantly he is the first Pope to choose the name of the great saint of the poor, Francis of Assisi.

Though he is socially conservative, he relates to people and their problems with astonishing ease. Recently a young divorced woman, who had been made pregnant by a married man, wrote to the Pope, asking such questions as would the Church baptise her child? She was amazed when a few days later her phone rang and a voice said 'This is Pope Francis'. He went on to say that if she could not find a priest to baptise her child, 'you know there is always me.'

This is a Pope whose vision stretches beyond Roman Catholics, beyond Christians, beyond believers of any sort: he wrote to an Italian newspaper saying that non-believers who followed their consciences would be forgiven by God. He also endeared himself to many by opposing the prospect of US intervention in Syria, saying: 'Violence and war are the language of death.' Perhaps we should not be surprised that his recent visit to Brazil attracted 3 million young people to a Mass celebrated on Copacabana beach, many of whom had spent the night in a vigil led by him. Or that *Time* magazine named him as their person of the year 2013.

Despite remarkable people like these Christian leaders, it seems impossible to deny that western Christianity is dying. The social historian Callum Brown gives Britain a curious distinction by writing that: '… the culture of Christianity has gone in the Britain of the new millennium. Britain is showing the world how religion as we have known it can die.'[6]

Religion as we have known it might be dying, but some of its elements are taking surprising new forms. In Cambridge, Massachusetts there are regular meetings of the Humanist Community at Harvard. The people who gather together are referred to as the 'congregation', there is a 'chaplain' who 'preaches'; the plate is passed to collect offerings and they sing cheerful and uplifting songs. It is in most outer ways a church, yet God is absent. It is as if the archetypes of community,

---

[6] Callum Brown, *The Death of Christian Britain: Understanding Secularization 1800–2000* (Routledge, 2001), p.198.

instruction, charitable giving and praise remain, but where is the central, motivating spirit? It is not God, or any aspect of God that so-called 'religious people', would recognise. The founder of this community, the Humanist chaplain Greg Epstein, decided to use words like 'congregation' because they evoke a close-knit community; he believes, 'We can learn from the positive while learning how to get rid of the negative.'[7]

His example has been followed by Jerry DeWitt, an evangelical minister who became an atheist and is building an atheist church in Louisiana, where he wants people to be part of a family; in the United Kingdom the Sunday Assembly draws people to godless meetings in a deconsecrated church in North London. Here they plan community functions, pass round a cup of wine and the founder, Sanderson Johns, shakes the hand of everyone as they leave in true Church of England style. Their mantra is: 'Live better, help often, wonder more.'

By the end of 2013, inspired by the Sunday Assembly Missionary Tour, satellite congregations were being formed in more than twenty cities in Britain and around the world. As Alain de Botton, one of the most forthright atheists in the United Kingdom, writes, 'rather than mocking religions, agnostics and atheists should instead steal from them, because they are packed with good ideas about how we might live and arrange our societies'.[8] Or, you could say, they are taking the archetypes and depriving them of their essence – or at the very least changing that essence.

So while attendance at the churches who believe in God shrinks every year, a godless church, using the age-old forms of worship without God, is growing.

---

[7] 'Church without God', Dan Merica CNN, http://religion.blogs.cnn.com/2013/06/22/church-without-god-by-design/
[8] Alain de Botton, *Religion for Atheists: A Non-Believer's Guide to the Uses of Religion* (Penguin, 2013).

So is the Britain of the twenty-first century finally without a God? Does it mean anything that the House of Commons continues a tradition begun in the sixteenth century and starts every sitting with a prayer?

> Lord, the God of righteousness and truth, grant to our Queen and her government, to Members of Parliament and all in positions of responsibility, the guidance of your Spirit. May they never lead the nation wrongly through love of power, desire to please, or unworthy ideals but laying aside all private interests and prejudices keep in mind their responsibility to seek to improve the condition of all mankind; so may your kingdom come and your name be hallowed. Amen.

My feeling is that such a prayer calls forth some deep response in us, whether we are believers or not. Parliament would be the poorer without these opening words. It is imbued with the language of spirituality – seeking the guidance of the Spirit, warning of the love of power and the desire to please, mindful of the risks of personal prejudice – perhaps most of all, looking to a divine kingdom, wanting the name of the divine to be held sacred. Yet it is couched in the language of the institution, the Church, the monarchy, and of course Parliament. It is one of the lingering reminders that Christianity is still the established religion of Great Britain, with the Queen at its head.

If it is true that, to all intents and purposes, the culture of Christianity has left Britain – and it seems clear that it has – then, in the spirit of the saying that 'nature abhors a vacuum', the space has been filled. It has been filled by spirituality. The most frequently heard statement on questions of belief is 'I am not religious, I am spiritual'. It has been suggested that a fifth of people in the UK fall into this category and a *Newsweek* survey in 2005 put the figure in the United States at a quarter. It is now a major strand of belief in the West. I think I might, with reservations, say it of myself.

What then, is meant by being spiritual rather than religious? The word 'religious' comes from the Latin *re-ligare*, to bind back, hence to bind back to one's source. To be religious implies belonging to an institution, holding to an organised collection of beliefs. Religion has stories, symbols, sacred places, clergy, rituals, festivals. It differs from private belief in that it is, as the French sociologist Émile Durkheim said, 'something eminently social'.[9] There are, according to some estimates, 4,200 religions in the world.

Religion of course includes spirituality. But what is spirituality on its own, without the support of a religious organisation? Those who call themselves spiritual rather than religious say that it is about a personal experience of a higher reality, rather than a blind faith in someone else's theories. It can include pagans, reflexologists, astrologers, homeopaths, reiki practitioners, devotees to healing crystals; it can include people with no specific spiritual practice, but who simply 'have a feeling that there must be something else', people who wish to contemplate the marvels of life on earth. It can include people who almost fall into the categories of double or multiple belonging, but who do not feel they can commit, even partially, to any faith. People who call themselves spiritual have one thing in common – they find their relationship to the world is filled with awe and wonder.

---

[9]   Émile Durkheim, *The Elementary Forms of the Religious Life* (*Les formes élémentaires de la vie religieuse*) 1912.

Even though the words 'spiritual but not religious' are said so often that for some they have become almost a cliché, the concept should not be dismissed out of hand. It is about things that cannot be expressed in words, it covers those mysterious areas of the non-conceptual. A practitioner of mindfulness meditation, which appeals to both churchgoers and to those who seek spirituality on its own, says:

> We're not worshipping a God or paying homage to something in the sky. It's about learning to accept things like impermanence and living in the moment. If you get a glimpse of how happy you can be by embracing the moment, all the chattering of your life stops.[10]

But the distinction between being religious and being spiritual cannot be drawn with the accuracy of a knife cutting butter, for the importance of living in the present is a belief also widely held by religious believers – one only has to consider Brother Lawrence's *The Practice of the Presence of God*, *The Eternal Now* of Paul Tillich, or, more recently, *We Walk the Path Together* by the Dominican Friar Brian Pierce. I think the most accurate distinction between religion and spirituality, certainly one that appeals to me, is: 'Religion asks you to learn from the experience of others. Spirituality urges you to seek your own.'[11]

Can one claim that spirituality is 'better' than religion or that religion is 'better' than spirituality?   I came across one experience that seems to indicate that there are moral judgments here, lingering in the differences between spirituality in the context of religion and spirituality on its own. Two academics, researching this subject, found that:

---

[10] Gaetan Louis de Canonville quoted in http://www.bbc.co.uk/news/magazine.

[11] From an interview quoted in *The Spiritual Revolution - why religion is giving way to spirituality,* Heelas and Woodward (Blackwell, 2005), p.12.

As we pushed open the doors of the churches, chapels and meeting houses on consecutive Sunday mornings, we became aware of a similarity that overrode all other differences. To step into a worship service is to find one's attention being directed away from oneself towards something higher. By contrast ... to enter into the holistic milieu is to find attention directed towards oneself and one's inner life.[12]

If this is generally true, then there seems no escaping a moral judgement implicit in the distinction.

All the major religions have, of course, their own spirituality, their own spiritual traditions. Nevertheless, despite such towering spiritual figures as Teresa of Avila, John of the Cross, Meister Eckhart and Thomas Merton, people today do not necessarily associate Christianity with spirituality. How can spirituality and religion be brought closer together? What is it, indeed, that is dividing them, leading people to say they are not religious, but they are spiritual?

There are almost as many answers to these questions as there are people who make the distinction and come down on the side of spirituality. So I shall look at one response to this dilemma – my own.

I would dearly love to belong to a religion, to give myself to it heart and soul and to find all the answers to my questions in one tradition. I have tried many times, but, in the end, I have failed. I cannot give myself heart and soul to one tradition to the exclusion of others.

---

12   Ibid. pp.13-14.

As I was for some years a Roman Catholic I was, like thousands of others, including many who have remained faithful, exasperated with its teaching on contraception, abortion and compulsory celibacy, embarrassed by the behaviour of some of its practitioners, even of its priests, and saddened that, though there is a strong mystical tradition in Christianity, it is so little taught, so little in evidence in the churches and Christian groups I have attended. The Church is an institution run by ordinary human beings, so we should not be too shocked that it has ordinary human failings, but my inability to remain a churchgoing Roman Catholic is not only that I am sometimes shocked and disappointed at what I find, it is that other music steals into my ears and draws me away.

There is the wisdom of the great world religions like Buddhism, Christianity, Judaism, Islam and Hinduism, but there are many less familiar areas where jewels of wisdom may be found – Sufism, Sikhism, the Zorastrian Scriptures, and individuals like Rabindranath Tagore, Ramakrishna and Rumi. For me a favourite source is Taoism, which says, for instance, that, 'He who knows, does not speak. He who speaks, does not know.' I do not know, so perhaps I can use this ignorance to justify my attempt to speak, for there is sometimes a temptation to try to communicate the incommunicable. It is an attempt to pin down the butterfly, while longing for it to live in its freedom and glory. Yet the mystery disappears from our grasp even as we seek to capture and express it.

Perhaps a good way to mark my own position in this elusive field is to tell the story from the Upanishads in which a father tried to teach his son about God. He told his son to put salt in water and come and see him the next day. He came, and together they looked into the water but could not see the salt, for it had dissolved. So his father said: 'Taste the water from this side. How is it?'

'It is salt.'

'Taste it from the middle. How is it?'

'It is salt.'

'Look for the salt and come and see me again.'

The son did so, saying, 'I cannot see the salt. I can see only water.'

His father then said: 'In the same way, O my son, you cannot see the Spirit. But in truth he is here. An invisible and subtle essence is the Spirit of the whole universe. That is Reality. That is Truth. THOU ART THAT.'

'Explain more to me, father.'

'So be it, my son.'[13]

Or, as the Judeo-Christian tradition has it, 'I am that I am.' As so often happens, a truth first glimpsed in another religion is there, firmly at the heart of Christianity.

Though I suppose I have to put myself in the group that says it is spiritual rather than religious, I still find there are elements of worship and ritual that I value and that I find most easily in Roman Catholicism. To sit, as I did for so long, in the body of a Dominican church is, time and time again, to be moved by the patient, regular attendance of the friars, providing a support and inspiration to my dilatory attendance; by the ritual, the appeal to the senses of sound and smell – I never fail to be moved by plainsong and the smell of incense. Most of all by the timeless words and actions of the Mass. I sometimes wish I still went to Mass and wonder when, or even if, this equivocation will be resolved.

---

13 *The Upanishads*, Chandogya Upanishad, trs. Juan Mascaro, p.118.

'In My End is My Beginning'

So where am I now, well into the second decade of the twenty-first century? Am I still looking or have I found? Maybe I have found something, but not in the way for which I hoped, vague though even that was. The curious part is that I am not really looking any more. Sometimes there is a new realisation – a whiff here, a glimpse there – an apprehension of how life could be – how in fact life *is* – if we were not so involved in our selves and our own little lives and our own little worlds. Rather like an animal scenting the air. Or a bird listening to a call. The silent melody sings on.

However in the interests of truth and of completing my story, there is more to be said, for this is not just my story, it is my story in the context of my time; I am simply one of many people who find themselves on a comparable journey. And like many of us, I have to admit I am no longer a Mass-going Roman Catholic. I wanted to be, and for many years I was, but increasingly I had to admit I was wobbling, ripe for falling. My final admission of defeat was caused by a scandal in the church of immense proportions. It was in 2010, when the news broke that more than half of the Catholic priests who had been convicted for child abuse over the previous decade and given prison sentences of at least a year, remained in the priesthood, with some still receiving financial support from the Church, even living in church houses. The Church, it was clear, appeared to be condoning their behavior.

The paedophilia scandal was not new – the news of priests abusing altar boys had been shocking us for some time as one by one the cases were reported – but this was too much. That these convicted men should still serve as priests and that the Church itself should seek to cover up their crimes was intolerable.

It was curious that I did not immediately say, as I know many did, 'That's it. I cannot any longer go to church or even attempt to be a Catholic.' It crept up on me. I just found that whereas I had been going regularly to the evening Mass at my local church, I was not going. One Sunday, two Sundays, then a third – I was somehow too busy or was prevented in some way from carrying out what had become my normal practice. Eventually I realised what was happening, what in fact had happened. I could no longer consider myself a member of the Roman Catholic Church. The scandal of the paedophile priests and the Church's attitude to them was the last straw. And in ceasing to call myself a Catholic, so I – unreasonably I think – felt uneasy at thinking of myself as a Christian. I could have returned to the Anglican Church, the tradition of my childhood, the Christianity I had tried for so long to regard as my faith, but somehow my attempts to be a Christian were over. Even though I love and admire the teaching of Christ, even though I am steeped in the traditions of Christianity, I can no longer call myself a Christian. There. I have said it. It was hard.

Facing this decision took time, but more shocks were to come. Barely had I accepted this conclusion, when I read a newspaper report that the Archbishop of Westminster, who though sympathetic to homosexual relationships was a leading figure in the campaign against same sex marriage, had banned the so-called 'Soho Masses', masses which had caused outrage in Rome, but had given comfort to many. These Masses had been going for six years – they were set up by a group of openly gay Catholics and sympathetic priests for those 'struggling to live within a church that takes an absolutist line against same-sex relationships.'[1] The decision seemed quite unambiguous. The Masses went against the Church's views on homosexuality, so they must stop. Fuel was being piled on to my defection and the flames of my anger burned higher.

I think however, I had got it wrong. I learnt later that the Masses had indeed got rather out of hand and that people were demonstrating outside the church; there was a feeling that something had to be done. And that in any case the decision to stop the Masses came on orders from Rome so there has to be some sympathy for the situation in which Westminster found themselves. A compromise was agreed. The church where the Masses were held, Our Lady of the Assumption in Warwick Street, was handed over to the care of the Ordinariate – the body set up by Rome to cater for Anglo-Catholics who have defected from the Church of England. And the gay Catholics who had been attending the Masses were encouraged to go to Farm Street Church, in Mayfair.

Hot on the heels of the banning of the Soho Masses at the beginning of 2013 came the news that a million anti-gay marriage postcards were handed out at Catholic Masses. The recipients were to sign them and send them to their local MPs asking them to vote against the Government's Equal Marriage Bill. Whatever views individuals may hold on this matter, surely it is not the Church's job to campaign? And is it in the spirit of Christ to use the celebration of the Eucharist as their campaigning ground?

Is this the Church founded by the man who preached love? A Church that excuses the abuse of children, appears to discourage people of the same sex who live together from celebrating Mass and organises their congregations in campaigns against equality? My decision was endorsed as I joined the great mass of people who can no longer tolerate the institutional Church.

---

[1] Jerome Taylor, *Independent*, 9 January 2013.

Am I then an atheist, a secularist? Most certainly not. Like so many others I am preoccupied by spirituality, the vibrant core at the heart of everything, but, again like so many others, I find it hard to accept what humankind and our institutions are doing to the spirit, the intangible, elusive spirit. I rejoice in wisdom wherever I find it, and this, while undoubtedly to be found in Christianity, seems so often to be in the spirituality of the East. So I stand to be accused of 'pick and mix' spirituality. I appreciate the dangers in this position and once tried to defend it. I don't bother any longer. There is such richness in so many traditions – why should we not take the wings of the morning and fly with them? We may be lucky enough to find a flower on which we can rest, where we can stay and live out our spiritual practice.

Others have held this belief with conviction and courage. The great Raimon Panikkar had a good start in crossing what many see as boundaries, having been born of a Spanish Roman Catholic mother and an Indian, Hindu, father – he called himself a Hindu-Christian priest. He made his first trip to India in 1954, when he met several western monks seeking eastern forms for the expression of their Christian beliefs, and later said: 'I left Europe [for India] as a Christian, I discovered I was a Hindu and returned as a Buddhist without ever having ceased to be Christian.'[2]

In the same spirit, twenty years later, the Benedictine Bede Griffiths, who spent half a lifetime in India, urged us to discover different aspects of truth and unite them in ourselves. 'I have to be a Hindu, a Buddhist, a Jain, a Parsee, a Sikh, a Muslim, and a

---

[2] This has been so often quoted that a source is no longer given.

Jew, as well as a Christian, if I am to know the Truth and to find the point of reconciliation in all religion.'[3]

They were prophets of our time, these men. Two great Christian spiritual leaders who experienced the interconnectedness of religions, yet died as Christians. Once again I am reminded of the poem I came across in India in 1993, 'There are many ways up a mountain.' Surely these are the voices to which we should listen, rather than to those whose policies create divisions and exaggerate difference?

As great leaders do, Bede Griffiths and Raimon Panikkar both reflected and led. Many of us had been living with these ideas, but often tentatively, flavoured with confusion, in my own case even with the hangover of a Protestant upbringing – guilt. (This is, I know, more often attributed to a Roman Catholic childhood, but it seemed to flourish equally in the milder climes of my own Anglican upbringing.) Human beings need traditions, we need rituals. Having cast ourselves out of our own traditions, where could we find them? For the moment, it seems, many of us have to learn to live without these supports. But a spiritual life not rooted in any tradition, any practice, any group, can be a lonely affair, hard to pursue enthusiastically. We need to belong to a group of like-minded people. We need each other. How do we survive spiritually, those of us who are passionately concerned with the spiritual life but who do not have a particular tradition? It is a question, I think, with as many answers as there are people asking it. I am one of the lucky ones, who have found a spiritual home in Zen. I live in Oxford and I have never ceased to wonder that Zen practice, complete with Sister Elaine MacInnes, a roshi who is also a practising Christian, should come to my doorstep.

---

[3] Bede Griffiths, *Return to the Centre* (Collins, 1976), p.71.

Very early on we were told that we should not write or speak about Zen until we had practised for thirty years. I can see why this restriction is imposed, for Zen evades words more completely than any other spiritual discipline I know; I am also deeply relieved, for having practised it for less than twenty years I am spared the impossible task of trying to describe it in depth. So all I shall say is that it is wonderful, infuriating, simple, complex, mind-blowing, exasperating and tough: it has shafts of pure joy and ease; it is as elusive as a beautiful scent, as complex as a spider's web. It is also painful – sitting for hours at a time cross-legged and unsupported – a practice age and a bad back has forced me to give up. Along with a few others in our group, I now sit demurely in a chair – and still get backache!

Zen is very strict, mostly silent. It has its own rituals and procedures, designed so that every meditator can be quiet and peaceful. We wear black – or at least dark colours that do not catch the eye and disturb those who are sitting with us – and sit in straight lines, facing the wall; after 25 minutes silence we rise and walk slowly round the room to ease aching legs, a practice known as kinhin, then return to our places. The normal practice is three 'sits', separated by kinhin, followed by a break – often for a meal. On retreats it is normal to do up to eight hours of sitting a day.

The setting is highly disciplined. Shoes must be left outside the door, the cushions correctly aligned, the bells rung at precisely the right moment and – hardest of all for those with weak backs or stiff legs – absolute stillness must be maintained. The Zen masters used to say you should sit 'mountain still', for when the body is unmoving then it is easier for the mind to be quiet. It is a stern and demanding practice which might surprise those who consider meditation self-indulgent: Sister Elaine gave the lie to that idea by saying that after sitting, meditators should be 'shot off their cushions into the world of greed, anger and ignorance, injustice, poverty and pollution'.[4]

It is the deepest form of meditation that I know, as satisfying as it is endlessly frustrating. If I have missed a day's meditation, when I settle down for it the next day, it is like coming home. I rest in peace. And it can, I am sure, lead to oneness. Ruben Habito, another contemporary Christian Zen teacher, has said of Zen that it is 'an invitation to experience where God dwells.' It would be hard to imagine a more sublime goal.

❧

One aspect of Zen that wonderfully depicts the human being struggling towards enlightenment is the famous ox-herding pictures. They form a series of pictures and short poems illustrating the stages of enlightenment and believed to be based on the work of a Taoist scholar living sometime before the twelfth century. They are sometimes seen as a Zen Buddhist interpretation of the progress through the Mahayana sutras, but they have the strength of all great archetypes in allowing everyone to attempt to interpret them, to see them from wherever they have reached on the journey to enlightenment.

In the first picture a figure, often a small boy, is seen setting off in search of the ox, which is a metaphor for enlightenment, or the true self, and can be interpreted as the state of being fully human. The boy doesn't really know where to look; he searches aimlessly, the only sound being the sound of cicadas. He progresses, as Zen practitioners hope to do, through various stages, first finding the ox's footprints. This is a crucial moment for many people – we may long to follow a path but how do we find the right one? The figure, symbol of course for each one of us, then finds the bull, catches him, tames him and in great joy

---

[4] Elaine MacInnes, *Light Sitting in Light* (Fount, 1996), p.viii.

rides him home. Once home he finds stillness and then, in the eight stage, both bull and self are transcended and all is empty. This is usually depicted as a clear, empty, circle and in some versions is the end of our exploring. He is enlightened. He has arrived. He has found oneness. There are, however, versions in which there are two more scenes, to my mind presenting a more complete and satisfying whole. Once the goal has been reached the seeker, the little boy, reaches the Source, where again there is the sound of cicadas; then he returns to ordinary life. In the crowded marketplace he mingles with the human race, spreading enlightenment by his very being.

He is a full human being leading an ordinary human life. And as St Irenaeus so memorably said: 'The glory of God is a human being fully alive.'

I love this version, where enlightenment is part of humanity and the enlightened person, sometimes without even being aware of it, helps to enlighten others. And the cicadas, which are heard both at the start of the journey and at the end, speak for so much that is in Zen. They are symbols of immortality; they represent a carefree insouciance; they spend the summer singing rather than storing food, even at the risk of being hungry in winter. The cicada moults and leaves behind an empty shell, so is seen as a symbol of reincarnation; it is short-lived and so is a symbol of our swiftly passing lives on earth. In this repeated shedding of its shell the cicada symbolises the many stages of transformation that take place on the inner journey. Thus it is no accident that the cicada accompanies the boy in his search for the ox. The cicada speaks for Zen with the most gracious eloquence.

There are others who speak beautifully for Zen, notably Peter Mathieson, the American writer who became a Buddhist monk. 'In zazen,[5] all knowing falls away; we simply *are'*, he

---

[5] Seated meditation.

writes. 'And that is the enlightened state, whether or not the practitioner has had a so-called "enlightenment experience."'[6] And of his own experience he writes:

> There was no hallucination, only awe, 'I' had vanished and also 'I' was everywhere. Then I let my breath go, gave myself up to immersion in all things, to a joyous *belonging* so overwhelming that tears of relief poured from my eyes. For the first time since unremembered childhood, I was not alone, there was no separate 'I'. Wounds, anger, ragged edges, hollow places were all gone, all had been healed; my heart was the heart of all creation.[7]

Many people who practise Zen are also practising Christians and this is, to me, immensely reassuring. I have spent far too much of my life struggling to be a Christian to give it up easily and completely or to want to see my country deprived of the richness it can bring. Though Zen is now my practice, Christianity is my upbringing, my tradition, the spiritual milk on which I was raised. I am curious at my own reaction to the acceptance that I am no longer a practising Roman Catholic. Even as I make that statement, I am looking for signs of hope that Christianity is not dead. I *want* it to be a living thing and to flourish, just as part of me wants to believe.

However, despite our culture and our social services being rooted in Christianity, we have to accept that we are living in the post-Christian age. Over fifty years ago the phrase 'the death of God' entered our consciousness through a book written by

---

[6] Peter Matthieson, *Nine-Headed Dragon River: Zen Journals* (Shambhala, 1985), p.9.
[7] Ibid, p.21.

a French theologian[8] and the question has been debated ever since. But the figures do not always support the slogan; it seems that God is not dead. Certainly the Christian God is not dead. A recent census taken in the UK shows that while the number of people identifying with no religion has doubled, over half the population describe themselves as Christian. And figures recorded in the United States in 2012 show that nearly three-quarters of Americans considered themselves Christians.

The argument about figures can and will continue, but actions speak louder than numbers and while it is often hard to think of the United Kingdom as a Christian country, there is evidence of such life in our Christian roots that we have to think again. How, when one considers the rapture with which two very different visits to this country were greeted recently, can we think this is not a Christian country?

Who, for instance, would have expected Pope Benedict XVI to visit Great Britain, a country so recently found by his German cardinal to be 'aggressively secular'? And, considering the atheist Richard Dawkins had declared the Pope to be 'an enemy of the people', who would have expected that visit to be a huge personal success? Yet in September 2010 the Pope flew into Edinburgh, visiting Glasgow and Birmingham and London. He had an audience with the Queen at Holyrood House and met the Archbishop of Canterbury, the Prime Minister and senior representatives of other political parties. He spoke at London's Westminster Hall and attended a service at Westminster Abbey. And most surprisingly he was given the sort of welcome more normally associated with pop stars and royalty. There were 65,000 people at the open air mass in Bellahouston Park, 80,000 people attended the prayer vigil in Hyde Park. And down the flag-lined Mall there were 200,000 people applauding and cheering, while the anti-papal demonstrators a few streets

---

[8]   Gabriel Vahanian, *The Death of God* (1961).

away could only muster 6,000. In 2010 the papal visit was, by universal agreement, a resounding success.

But for me it was another visit the year before, in October 2009, that moved me to tears. A small casket containing a few bones from a thigh and a foot of a young girl toured England and Wales for four weeks, drawing huge crowds wherever it went. These were the bones of a French girl who died of tuberculosis, aged 24, in 1897; the remains of the Catholic saint, a French Carmelite nun, St Thérèse of Lisieux.

Oxford, where I live, was one of the places visited. I have never entered enthusiastically into the cult of relics and my years as a Roman Catholic came too late in my life for saints to have the meaning for me that they do for cradle Catholics. Nevertheless something drew me, and I was determined to go.

I couldn't understand why I was so nervous; I for whom the saints were not that important and who had never seen the point of worshipping relics. Was it simply that I knew there would be a lot of people there and that I must get there in plenty of time – a sort of urge to be there, whatever it was? I don't think so. It was more than that, but I didn't know what it was. Perhaps it was a conviction that something extraordinary was about to happen. So, as it was too wet to bike, I caught a bus, arriving at the church at 4.30, an hour and a half early as St Thérèse, or rather her bones, were not due to arrive until 6.00. Already the church was full to overflowing and people were queuing down the Woodstock Road. I just got a seat, on the back row on the left – it must have been almost the last one going. It was squashed and uncomfortable, I could barely squeeze in – never mind – I was there.

For half an hour or so I tried to pray, but it was uncomfortable and I was finding it hard. I was glad when someone started leading us in the rosary, grateful that we had something on which to focus our thoughts as we waited. It also seemed entirely appropriate for Thérèse, who must have said the rosary for hours during her short life.

Exactly on time, at 6 o'clock, the procession began, led by children scattering rose petals on the ground. There were priests young and old, ordinands, a few children – but not one woman in the procession – a sad reminder that the Roman Catholic Church is still a male-dominated organisation. Someone was throwing petals from the balcony above, clearly hoping to land some on the relic. A photographer downstairs understood her situation and waved to her to wait – then pointed when he saw the casket. She successfully landed a huge double handful of rose petals on the tiny casket.

At the back of the church as I was, I was one of the first to see the ornate casket, carefully cased in glass and carried by six strong men. And inside a few bones of a young French girl who died over a century ago.

I was moved beyond tears. This young girl loved God so well that here we were, priests and lay people alike, cramming the largest church in Oxford to welcome two or three bones. It was extraordinary. It was true. And we were right to be there. We were honouring a life of love, for those bones symbolised the innocence and purity of a life well lived; a life spent loving God.

I stayed for three hours and came back the next day for the Latin Mass that she would have known, but I could barely follow it, even with a pamphlet in Latin. I lit a candle for John, whose funeral had taken place in this same church, venerated the casket, thanking St Thérèse for being.

Clearly there are still occasions when Christianity seems to take us over once more, to rule our hearts, if not our heads. Once again I see myself as a child of my time; unable to call myself a Christian yet unable completely to leave its embrace.

In dropping out of regular churchgoing and in finding that I can no longer consider myself a real Christian, I do not find even the slightest change in my attitude to spiritual values. Rather it is those values that still draw me: the values themselves, drawing on the wisdom of all religions, but not seen through the eyes of any particular one. While love is the great container of all spiritual values, the context in which they must operate, there are three elements I find increasingly necessary: they are solitude, silence and stillness.

Solitude is the most ambivalent. Solitude, when it is experienced as loneliness, can be empty and terrifying. Nobody would deliberately seek the solitude of bereavement – the empty place at breakfast, the slippers never to be used again, facing the world as one person rather than as half a couple. It is a glass space, inhabited by every fear known to the lost mortal floundering in its grasp. I have experienced it for over twenty years and I have not yet become used to it. But even so, there are occasions when I long for solitude.

Paradoxical? Yes, of course. Surely a widow living alone has her fill of solitude? But solitude accepted, or solitude voluntarily sought is quite different to loneliness; it is benign and fruitful. To be deprived for too long of its necessary space is to be hungry when there is no food, thirsty when there is not even a muddy pool from which to drink. It may not be an easy option, but periods of solitude are for many a necessity. Solitude is needed if the inward eye is to be allowed to open: crowds, incessant busyness and noise make the spirit shrink as surely as the tentatively extended horns of a snail will flinch when touched.

Yet here too there are dangers. As those of us who live alone leave a noisy party, looking forward to the peace of our own homes, are we not running away from people and seeking the comfort of having no one to please, no one to stop one doing precisely what one chooses? Solitude can be self-serving and selfish and those of us who need solitude have to remember that. Yet, if we are to grow inwardly, if we are to be in any way creative, we do need periods of solitude. To reach that state of oneness where there is no other, we need periods of solitude. Solitude which allows the self to merge with infinite being.

Thomas Merton, who was well acquainted with solitude, regarded it as quite simply essential:

> Without solitude of some sort there is and can be no maturity. Unless one becomes empty and alone, he cannot give himself in love because he does not possess the deep self which is the only gift worthy of love. And this deep love, we immediately add, cannot be *possessed*. My deep self is not 'something' which I acquire, or to which I 'attain' after a long struggle. It is not mine, and cannot become mine. It is no 'thing' - no object. It is 'I'............. This 'I' is Christ Himself, living in us; and we, in Him, living in the Father.[9]

To be alone with God is to have the chance to find one's true self.

Is silence any more natural than solitude? Probably not. Yet most people, and especially people drawn to some form of spiritual life, find they need periods of both.

Silence and solitude swim in the same waters, as close as sisters. And like sisters, they also have their own qualities.

Silence is an aspect of wisdom, indeed the philosopher Wittgenstein's favourite aphorism was 'Whereof one cannot speak, thereof one should be silent.' No doubt he knew of Lao Tsu's famous lines: 'He who speaks does not know. He who

---

[9] *Notes for a Philosophy of Solitude: Disputed Questions* (Farrar, Straus & Cudahy, 1960). Quoted in Thomas Merton, *Essential Writings* (Orbis, 2004).

knows does not speak.' The wise are not chatterboxes. If I were wise I would not be writing this, but my need to work out what I think and feel is greater than my discretion.

True silence is more, much more, than the absence of sound – it is a state of mind and heart. It need not be dour and remote. I was told a charming story of Abhishiktananda, at a time when he was keeping strict silence. On his walks along the banks of the Ganges he sometimes passed another *sadhu*, who was also in silence. They would smile radiantly at each other, making expansive gestures sharing the beauty of the world, their joy in the river and their love of God. Neither spoke, but they could not pass each other without acknowledging each other and their joy. This same person, Abhishiktananda, also loved to talk and he was realistic about his capacity for silence. One of his friends said of him, presumably speaking of times when he was *not* in silence: 'Now there's someone who can talk about silence for 24 hours a day!'

As with solitude, anyone seeking silence has to ask themselves whether they are wanting to escape from relationships. Yet it is perhaps inevitable that as our world becomes noisier so our need for silence grows greater. As silent meditation becomes increasingly popular and meditation groups spring up as fast as church pews empty, it is sad that many priests seem slow to realise how we, the people, long for more silence in church, temple and synagogue.

Perhaps the first sound coming from the everlasting silence was that sound known as 'the music of the spheres'. In the twentieth century the music of the spheres was re-created at the start of Bronowski's television series *The Ascent of Man*; it was a curious, whispering, mysterious, complex sound. It was some 35 years ago, yet I still remember it with a sense of familiarity. 'Yes,' I thought, 'that is what the music of the spheres must sound like, if only we could hear it.' This surely was 'the OM that time and history utter on their way, the OM uttered by Space when entering into time.'[10] As so often it is Meister Eckhart who has the last word. 'There is nothing so like God,' he said, 'as Silence.'

Silence and solitude can lead to the rare and exquisite quality of stillness. This is not a quality I can even hope to claim. When I was young I was an impatient fidget; even now I am the one who cannot stop picking at a bowl of nuts placed nearby; I catch myself longing for the end if a social occasion goes on too long. Stillness is a wonderful quality, sometimes found in people who, at some atavistic level, one knows to be holy. Such people are not rocked by events, they do not suddenly explode in anger, they seem content in a space which is both their own and cosmic. That space is past and future, it is here and there, it is north, south, east and west. They are the people who, as Ken Wilber says, 'walk very gently into the fog of the world, and transform it entirely by doing nothing at all'.[11] The people who can stand on the edge of the great void of unknowing and just 'be'. Sometimes they are people who emanate radiance and light and those in their presence never forget the experience of meeting them.

For most of us moments of stillness are rare, longed for and exquisite. They are beyond description, beyond words. When we are graced with them we find we are not trying to possess anything nor be anything. This place we are is here. The time we are in is now, and only now. Sometimes we feel this in unexpected, noisy moments, but usually we need times to withdraw, times to wander aimlessly, to watch and listen, to let go of our striving, if we are to glimpse this blessed state.

---

[10] Abhishiktananda, *Ascent to the Depth of the Heart* (ISPCK, 1998), p.190.
[11] Ken Wilber, *One Taste: Daily Reflections on Integral Spirituality* (Shambala, 2000), p.35.

Here, in this quiet abode, lives God. He is of course in the burning fiery furnace and in the eye of the storm, though these may not be places to which we would willingly travel. Stillness, however, is not only *where* he is but *what* he is. He is, as T. S. Eliot well knew, 'the still point of the turning world'. He is where the dance is.

❦

So where are we now, as the twenty first century continues its increasingly godless way? It seems that even as we embrace spirituality, so we reject religion and yet continue to try to define God. The only definition of God to which I am drawn is the God who is pure Being. Who is in the moment of birth and the moment of death; in washing the dishes; in standing still and in moving on. In energy, in loving, in listening … most of all in the present moment. The understanding of this idea of God as Being is the spirituality I seek, though how to define that word has defeated anyone who has ever attempted it. Enough to say that spirituality includes a search for wholeness. It is concerned with the sacred, the numinous, the quest for meaning, the mystical. And it is inseparable from the search for oneness.

The Beech Tree, gracing my life when I was a teenager, gave me my first glimpse of oneness, completeness. Years later, on a shamanic journey, the violin and bow that, without a player, were the source of sweet music, sang of the importance of letting things be, of getting myself out of the way. I come to agree with three of the people I most admire. Ramana Maharshi: 'The Self is not attained by doing anything other than remaining still and being as we are.' Eckhart Tolle: 'The ultimate truth of who you are is not I am this or I am that, but I am.'[12] Thomas Merton: 'Be what you are.'

---

[12] Eckhart Tolle, *A New Earth* (Michael Joseph, 2005), p.57.

These days I rarely feel acquisitive, never ambitious. Now, despite the loneliness of old age as, one by one, friends and family die; despite occasional depression, for the most part I am curiously content, curious because my content embraces pain and suffering and my own shortcomings. Enough to live in this moment, now. If I can live in this moment all will be well. I no longer mind if I don't understand.

Index